The Clipper Ship
Sebastopol

New Zealand Immigration Ship 1861—1863

By Belinda Lansley

*Ancestral Journeys
of New Zealand
Series*

This book would not have been possible without the help of the following people. Special thanks to:

Peter Dillon, Master Researcher
Graham and Bev Jones, for the John McLachlan diary
Roger Fyfe, Canterbury Museum
Klaus Nasterlack, Historian of Hohen-Sülzen, Germany
Gunter Flohn, Historian of Kindenheim, Germany
Ian and Stella Arnst, Christchurch German Researchers
Barbara Corrigan, Tisch family
Craig Hartwig, Zinckgraf family
Roy Little, Kippenberger family
Pip Grant-Taylor, Kissel family
Robert Kinsey, for law advice
Stuart Lansley, for editing my work
and Marolyn Diver of Dornie Publishing.

Dornie Publishing Company

Grasmere, Invercargill
www.dorniepublishing.tk

Original text © Belinda Lansley 2012
Images © named individuals, institutions
All rights reserved
ISBN 978-0-473-21890-4

Cover Design by Strawberrymouse Designs

Dedicated to Stuie, Maia, Arielle and Louis

Belinda Lansley

Great Great Great Granddaughter of Karl Philipp Meng and
Elise Katharina Ellenberger, *Sebastopol* passengers, 1863
and
Great Great Great Great Niece of William Lord, *Sebastopol* passenger, 1861

Contents

Introduction	7
The Ship	9
First Voyage to New Zealand 1861	27
Passengers on the First Voyage 1861	43
Second Voyage to New Zealand 1863	53
Passengers on the Second Voyage 1863	75
Passenger Lists	89
Bibliography	*110*

Introduction

This book covers the history of one of the lesser known ships that ferried migrants from Great Britain to New Zealand. As far as I know, this is the first time the whole story of the *Sebastopol* has been told in one place, as there are no known books or internet sites dedicated to the whole story of this ship.

This book almost didn't happen because of the Christchurch Earthquakes of 4 September 2010 and 22 February 2011, as most historical resources have been trapped in various buildings around Christchurch. It is only through the kindness of Graham and Bev Jones who sent me a copy of the one and only ship's diary for *Sebastopol*, that I was able to complete the book. Roger Fyfe from the Canterbury Museum then managed to get a clearer copy for me just as it was being moved to another location. Peter Dillon has also spent many hours looking up the *Sebastopol* on the internet and having chats with me on the email to ascertain the exact movements of this ship. His work has been invaluable and I cannot thank him enough.

All sources are referenced carefully at the back of this book. Some sources may have errors. Often in the past people exaggerated or made incorrect entries in the records. Advertisements for ships often made a ship sound better than it really was in order to gain passengers, just as advertisements operate these days. So I have worked with what was available and hope this written record is as accurate as possible.

There were not many accounts from this ship. If anyone has further information on the ship *Sebastopol* including ship diaries, family letters or comments in their family histories about the journey that you are willing to share, please contact me so it can be added to any future updated editions.

Belinda Lansley

belinda.lansley@yahoo.co.nz

The Ship

Construction of the Ship *Sebastopol*

The *Sebastopol* was built in 1854 or 1855 in New Glasgow, Nova Scotia, Canada by George Rogers McKenzie. It was registered in Pictou.[1] George Rogers McKenzie (1798–1876) was a ship builder, sea captain and politician who was known as the "father of shipbuilding" in Pictou County. He built many ships of a superior class and sold ships to the British and American armies for use in the Crimean and American Civil Wars respectively. He also supplied ships for the coal trade from Pictou to the United States as well as for the timber trade to Great Britain. His business flourished in the 1850s and 1860s.[2]

Clipper ship Lammermuir, which was built in 1856 and had a tonnage of 952 tons; similar statistics to the Sebastopol. Courtesy of Wikipedia. No picture has been found for the Sebastopol.

The *Sebastopol* was built from oak, tamarack, birch and pitch pine. In 1861 the ship was sheathed in felt and yellow metal. It was partly fastened with iron bolts. It had a weight of 992 tons[3] with a burden of 1800 to 2000 tons, depending on which advertisement you read. The weight of burden was a good guide as to the maximum cargo allowed on board that would make the journey economic, as well as making sure the weight was not exceeded, which could cause the ship to sink while at sea.[4]

The *Sebastopol* was a clipper ship. The name "clipper ship" was a synonym for a merchant ship. They were first created by American ship builders in the 1840s and were extra fast, travelling on average 250 miles per day while other types of ships averaged 150 miles per day. English ship builders started to build them as well. They revolutionised sea transport and were wonderful ships to behold. Clipper ships had three masts and square sails, and it was this combination that made them so fast and popular in the 19th century.[4]

The Name *Sebastopol*

The ship *Sebastopol* likely received its name from the Siege of Sevastapol (sometimes spelt Sebastopol) which lasted from September 1854 to September 1855 during the Crimean War.[5] The siege and the war in general would have been in the newspapers worldwide, and the place name Sebastopol would have been in common usage at the time the ship was being built.

Owners of the *Sebastopol*

The first owner of the *Sebastopol* was listed as "McKenzie," likely George McKenzie, the builder of the ship itself. There were probably many journeys for the *Sebastopol*, from 1855 onwards, likely around Canada and America where it was registered until 16 February 1859.[6] The ship would have then travelled from Canada to Great Britain where it was bought at some stage by Kidston & Co., a Glasgow based company. The ship was registered in Glasgow, in around 1859.[3] Kidston & Co. was run by the Kidston family of Glasgow, a family of merchants and shipowners.[7]

When Willis, Gann & Co. of London chartered the boat on two voyages to New Zealand in 1861 and 1863, it was still owned by Kidston & Co.[8]

Willis, Gann & Co.

Willis, Gann & Co. ran a line of packet ships from Great Britain to New Zealand in the early years of colonisation. A packet ship was originally used for shipping post office mail to the colonies and other places around the world, but this meaning was eventually extended to include passengers as well as mail.[9] Willis, Gann & Co. advertised regularly in English newspapers. The company was run by Arthur Willis, who was a Founding Director of the New Zealand Company of 1839 that promoted the colonisation of New Zealand.[10] He was also a representative of Lloyds and a member of the London Society of Shipowners. He encouraged famous people such as Dr Julius Haast to travel to New Zealand and explore the land.[11]

In 1854 the provincial governments became responsible for immigration. The Province of Canterbury had the largest immigration scheme of all the provinces, bringing in almost a fifth of all immigrants between 1858 and 1870. Two thirds of all passengers arriving in Canterbury were assisted; generally, half of their fare was paid by the Provincial Government.[12]

Willis, Gann & Co. had a general rate for charging passengers, but this changed every few years. In 1855–57 the going rate for a single farm labourer in steerage was £8[13], but this had increased to £13 10s by 1861, and for some reason then reduced to exactly £13 by 1863. In 1863, rival company Messrs. Shaw, Savill secured the contract for carrying emigrants to Otago, the fares being £12 from Glasgow and £13 10s from London.[14] They had the majority of the market at this time and maybe Willis and Gann were trying to compete with a small discount for passengers from London. In 1861 the rates for steerage passengers on the *Sebastopol* were as follows:

Single man or woman	£13 10s
Couple	£27
Child	£6 15s
Infant	free

In 1863 the rates for steerage passengers on the *Sebastopol* were as follows:

Single man or woman	£13
Couple	£26
Child	£6 10s
Infant	free

In the *Sebastopol* passenger lists there is no mention of the cost for cabin passengers. However for the *Clontarf* from 1855–57, Willis

Gann & Co. were charging £60 for one person in a chief cabin measuring 6 by 7ft, or £40 per person for two people sharing a cabin. The second cabins were 6ft 9in by 7ft 6 in and for four people this cost £25 per person. Also available were second cabins for married couples measuring 3ft 6in by 7ft 8in at £25 per person.[13] It is likely Willis, Gann & Co. would have charged higher prices for the *Sebastopol* in the 1860s.

The average annual wage for a housemaid in the 1850s-1860s was £11–£14.[15] Therefore the full cost of the journey was a full year's wage. The average annual wage for a farm labourer in England and Wales in 1860 was £30 2s 4p[16], so the full cost of the journey was over a third of their annual wage. We can now see that travel to New Zealand was expensive and what a struggle it was to raise even half the fare. They often had help from family and friends already in the colony and of course the Provincial Government assisted by paying part of the fare.

Life on Board a Clipper Ship

The Willis, Gann & Co. chart from the 1855–1857 period, on the following page shows the food allocated to the different classes of passengers.[13] The second cabin and steerage passengers were the only ones who received lime juice to keep away the scurvy. Maybe the first class passengers received enough vitamin C from the extra muscatel raisins that were served to them. Records show that sometimes fowl were kept in coups for fresh eggs, and sometimes larger animals were kept on board for fresh meat. Water was stored in barrels but became stale and often grew algae or had vermin fall in and die. Food was stored in lidded barrels but if someone left the lid off they could often become contaminated with rat and mice droppings. The bad hygiene often led to dysentery, cholera and many deaths on board. Flour often had weevils.

Illness was rife on some journeys, especially when steerage passengers were confined below decks during massive storms in the Southern Ocean. The ships were cleaned with vinegar and chloride of lime to remove vomit and make things smell better, while precious water was kept for drinking.

Weekly Dietary Scale for each Adult Passenger.

Articles.	Chief Cabin.	Second Cabin.	Steerage.
Preserved Meats	1½ lb.	1½ lb.	1 lb.
Preserved Salmon	½ ”	—	—
Assorted Soups	1 ”	—	—
Soup and Bouilli	—	½ lb.	—
York Ham	1 ”	½ ”	—
Tripe	½ ”	—	—
Fish	½ ”	¼ lb.	—
Prime India Beef	½ ”	1 ”	1¼ lb.
Irish Mess Pork	1 ”	1½ ”	1 ”
Biscuit	3 ”	4¼ ”	3½ ”
Flour	4¼ ”	4¼ ”	3 ”
Rice	1 ”	1 ”	½ ”
Barley	¼ ”	½ ”	—
Peas	½ pint	½ pint	½ pint
Oatmeal	½ ”	½ ”	1 ”
Preserved Milk	½ ”	—	—
Sugar, refined	½ lb.	—	—
Sugar, raw	¾ ”	1 lb.	1 lb.
Lime Juice	—	6 oz.	6 oz.
Tea	3 oz.	1½ oz.	1½ oz.
Coffee	5 ”	3 ”	2 ”
Butter	½ lb.	½ lb.	6 ”
Cheese	½ ”	¼ ”	—
Currants	¼ ”	¼ ”	—
Raisins, Valentia	½ ”	½ ”	½ lb.
Raisins, Muscatel	¼ ”	—	—
Suet	½ ”	6 oz.	6 oz.
Preserved Carrots	½ ”	—	—
Pickles	¼ pint	¼ pint	¼ pint
Vinegar	¼ ”	—	—
Mustard	½ oz.	½ oz.	½ oz.
Pepper	½ ”	¼ ”	¼ ”
Salt	2 ”	2 ”	2 ”
Potatoes, fresh or	3½ lb.	3½ lb.	2 lb.
Preserved ditto	½ ”	½ ”	½ ”
Water	28 quarts	21 quarts	21 quarts

Food chart for Willis, Gann & Co. from 1855–1857

Married couples' accommodation in steerage: bunks to the left and right; central table; light from the uncovered hatch. (London Illustrated News, 13 April 1844)

Toileting on ships was not pleasant. Often pieces of rag, soaked in vinegar, were hung on the back of the toilet door. These were used to wipe with and were shared over and over, often leading to dysentery! The sewage was often flushed into the bilge with buckets of water until emptied at port. The bilge was below steerage so the stench was not pleasant. People would be horrified these days but back then hygiene was generally not understood.[17]

The sleeping arrangements were bunk beds for steerage, with single women and single men having their own areas. Families often became separated as most of the time children over the age of 12 were transferred to the single men's or single women's quarters. Bedding was aired in fine weather but often became soaked if water was coming into the ship; this led to influenza and pneumonia outbreaks.[17]

Some ships were better managed than others. The low death count on the *Sebastopol's* journeys suggests good management, and maybe reasonably good weather, but also some good luck that a major outbreak of illness didn't happen during the journeys. The Commissioners in 1861 were happy with the health of the passengers, the cleanliness of the ship and the stores of food, showing good management of the ship. The second journey in 1863 had no deaths at all, which was virtually unheard of in the 1860s.

On the more positive side, a ship journey such as this would have been one of life's biggest adventures for the emigrants. They would see and experience things they never dreamed of, including strange sea creatures, new constellations in the skies and a sea voyage which most would never repeat again in their lifetime, culminating in a strange new land at the final port. At night the passengers entertained each other with music, lectures of the new country and games, made new friends and contacts and looked forward to a brighter future in their new country.

Crew of a Clipper Ship

The average crew of a clipper ship without migrants was about 17, including the Captain, First Mate (or Chief Officer), Second Mate, Midshipman (Apprentice Officer), Ship's Carpenter, Boatswain, 9-10 ordinary seamen and the Cabin Boy who was used for mundane duties. There were usually two cooks: the Passenger's Cook who made food for the steerage passengers; and the Ship's Cook for the cabin passengers and crew, who catered for their more refined tastes.

The crew numbers became closer to 40 when emigrants were on board, with additional crew being the Ship's Surgeon and Constable to keep the passenger welfare attended to. A Schoolmaster was on board, to teach the children and a Matron to separate the single women from the single men. Sometimes there was a Minister on board. The records for *Sebastopol* mention a Third Mate, an Apprentice and also a Steward. There were usually several Stewards who looked after the Cabin Passengers. Some people took up a job on board to get free passage out.[18] The Matron was often a woman looking to emigrate who took on the job in exchange for free passage.

Wages for the crew were on average £7 per month on the way to New Zealand with good food and comfortable accommodation but up to £100 wage for the home journey, to ensure crew stuck with the ship and didn't desert once in New Zealand. Even with the better wage desertions were common.[18]

The Ship

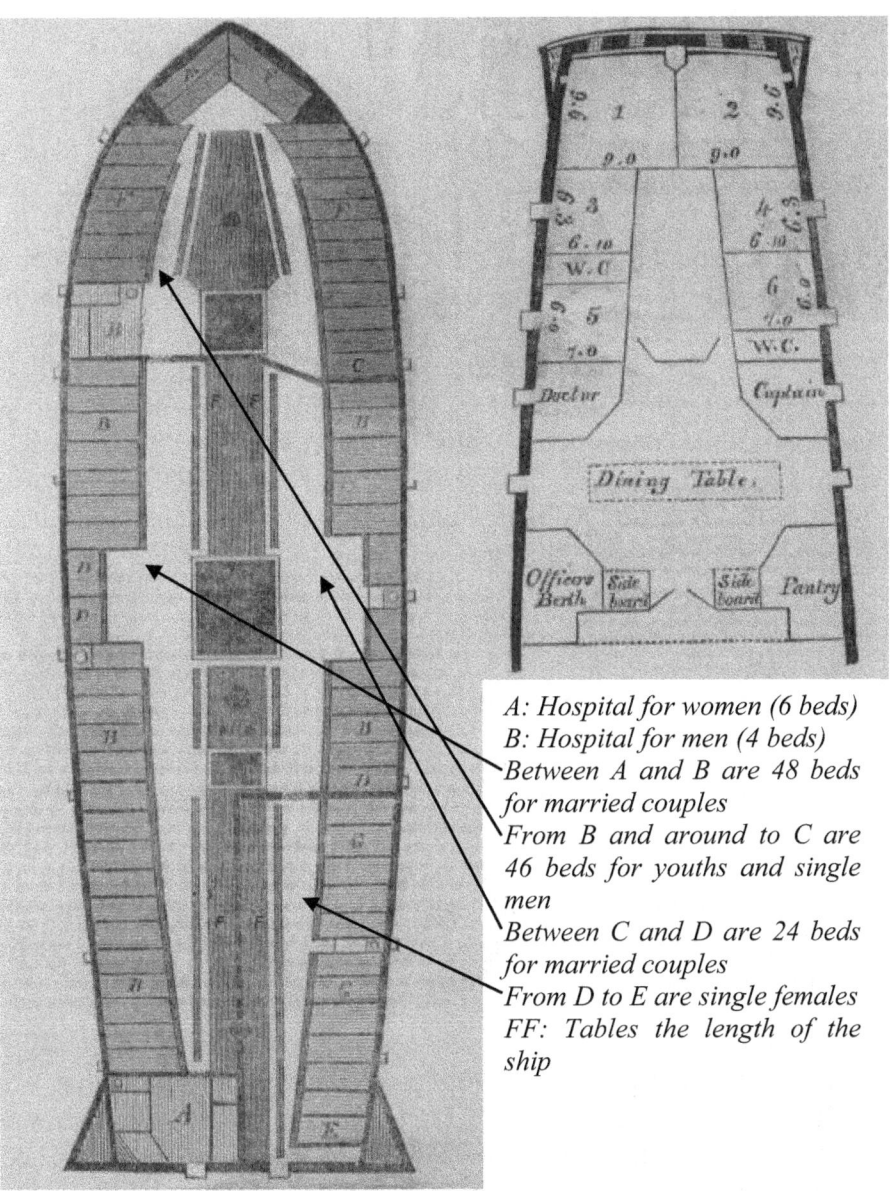

A: Hospital for women (6 beds)
B: Hospital for men (4 beds)
Between A and B are 48 beds for married couples
From B and around to C are 46 beds for youths and single men
Between C and D are 24 beds for married couples
From D to E are single females
FF: Tables the length of the ship

Plan of Emigrant Ship Between Decks (left) and Plan of Cabin Accommodation (right) (courtesy London Illustrated News)

The First Known Journey of the *Sebastopol*

The first journey that has been found for the *Sebastopol* is a journey from Gravesend leaving 23 March 1859[19] to Hobson's Bay, Melbourne, Australia arriving 8 July 1859.[20] There was one passenger on board, Mr. L. Vaughan.[19] It then sat in port while the cargo was removed. On 12 August 1859 the ship was noted as being 992 tons and the captain was J. A. Fraser, the same captain as the first journey to New Zealand two years later. De Pass Brothers and Co were the agents for the cargo that was on board.[21] The cargo included a grand piano that Mr. Richard Paling was advertising in Melbourne newspaper, The Argus, on 14 July 1859 as well as other instruments and music.[22] In The Argus on 18 July 1859 there was a lot of food advertised as being "ex-*Sebastopol*" including 1050 bags of oats.[23] It seems that this trip was mainly a freighting trip. The ship left port for Guam in the Pacific Ocean, north of Papua New Guinea on 15 August 1859.

Other Ships Named *Sebastopol*

There was a barque of 609 tons called *Sebastopol* that made many trips between Australia and London and other destinations. There was a trip to Australia at almost the exact same time as the 992 ton *Sebastopol* so care has been taken on the research for this book, not to confuse the two ships with each other. A barque is normally a vessel of three or more masts, square rigged on all masts except for the aftermost which is fore and aft rigged.

On 11 June 1859 there was a newspaper report of a ship called *Sebastopol*, a barque of 609 tons captained by Dawson, that was loading for Sydney at London.[24] On the journey to Sydney there was a fight on the high seas on 15 July 1859 where Chief Officer William Mitchell had to say to John Boyce two or three times that the ship was going to windward. John retorted back that William "didn't need to chaw that over so," and hit the Chief Officer "without further reason." Boyce was to be imprisoned and kept to hard labour for 14 days.[25] On 15 August 1859 the *Sebastopol* arrived in Sydney from London,[26] exactly the same date that the 992 ton clipper ship *Sebastopol* departed Melbourne. The smaller sized ship had a cargo of £18,643.[27] On 18 October 1859 Messrs Bowden and Threkeld advertised that a two third share in the ship was to be sold on 21 October 1859. It stated that the ship was built in Quebec in about 1854 of "very superior timber known as Tamarack".[28] On 26 October 1859 it was reported that the sale of shares made £1,500.[29] The final report on this ship stated that on 19 February 1860 the *Sebastopol* was sailing from Newcastle, NSW to San Francisco with a cargo of 800 tons of coal when it was wrecked at the Chatham Islands. Captain Thomas James McGrath and his family and crew all got off the ship safely, but the barque was broken in three pieces.[30]

As well as the barque *Sebastopol* there were many other ships with the same name of a different rigging or design and sailing in different waters or in a different time period to the 992 ton *Sebastopol*. One boat named *Sebastopol* was wrecked on 18 September 1855 in Lake Michigan, coming into Milwaukee with six lives lost. It was a wooden side-wheel steamer, 230 foot, 863 tons, built in 1855 at Cleveland, Ohio. Its paddlewheels were fifty feet in diameter. It was in its first year of operation.[31]

There was also a French Navy owned warship the *Sebastopol* minesweeper, that was built in November 1918. It was nearly lost in a storm in Lake Superior in 1918 on its maiden voyage. Two other minesweepers, the *Inkerman* and *Ceriosoles,* disappeared on the same journey, but *Sebastopol* managed to stay upright. It sailed for many years before being wrecked in 1933 off Cape St Francis.[32]

Chinese Immigration and the *Sebastopol*

On 23 December 1860 a ship called *Sebastopol* of 938 tons departed from Canton (Xiamen), China, full of Chinese immigrants. It arrived at Georgetown, British Guiana (Guyana) on 28 March 1861.[33] This journey fits in between the ship's first trip to Australia in 1859 and the first trip with immigrants to New Zealand, leaving 5 September 1861. Other ships that did the London to Lyttelton run also did a similar trip laden with Chinese immigrants. One of these ships was the *Mystery,* which sailed under the flag of Willis, Gann & Co.

So it is highly likely that this *Sebastopol* was the clipper ship of 992 tons, but with its weight recorded incorrectly. The weight for the *Mystery* was also incorrect – it was recorded as weighing 1074 tons[33] instead of the usual 1069 in most records.[34]

In 1834 slavery was abolished and the mainly African slaves who had been freed chose to live off the fertile land in British Guyana and take less paid work, which meant there were fewer workers for the plantations. Sugar plantation owners gained new workers from Portugal, India and some from China. The Chinese workers were mainly travelling under a contract of indenture.

There were 39 ships that brought the Chinese labourers to British Guyana. They were chartered by recruiting agents based in Canton, China, with the cost of shipping shared between the colony's immigration fund and the plantation owners. The ships travelled via Singapore and Cape Town, arriving at Georgetown. The journey usually took between 70 and 177 days.[35]

The *Sebastopol* was carrying 283 men, 45 women, four boys and one girl, a total of 333 immigrants. When they disembarked in Georgetown however, there were 282 men, 42 women, four boys and one girl, a total of 329 immigrants with one man and three women dying on the 95 day voyage. This was a low percentage of deaths for the number of passengers on board.

An excerpt from a letter written aboard the ship *Mystery* by Rev. William Lobschied on 29 May 1861 gives an insight into some of the passengers on these journeys in general and the state of health they were sometimes in:

"At least two thirds of the men on board were opium smokers; but it being cold and the deck always occupied by the crew — in the discharge of their duty, I did not like to force everybody on deck until we should have set sail. Then after our departure from Hong Kong I tried to get the men on deck, I could hardly believe my eyes, for I fancied myself in the most disgusting outskirt of a large Chinese town with scenes of misery around me which defy description. Men teeming with vermin, full of sores about them, emaciated so as to consist of nothing but bone and skin, scaly and spotted all over from

former diseases, three in four full of itch in its most loathsome state, dirty as if they had never seen water, and dull from opium smoking, some of them so weak that they would cry like children when being called to me and wash themselves. I need hardly add that I regretted having undertaken a duty so desperate and hopeless, being sure that every gale would demand its victims from a crowd that had grown old at the age of from 25–35, ruined their digestive organs, who could not breathe without the poisonous drug, and were too weak to withstand a single day's starvation from sea-sickness. Ninety of these men had paid from $15–$18 each to the Portuguese and a crimp of the name of Nung from Sinning, they had no money left for purchasing any refreshment. Hence many of them had sold their clothing and were now lying there in the miserable rags in which they had first presented themselves; yea one of them had not even a pair of trousers and, could hardly be got to move, which alone disclosed the shocking state he was in. . . . The rest, who are bona fide emigrants from the Country, are in general in a very good state of health, and will prove to be useful Colonists"

Another passage from the *Royal Gazette* in Guyana of 29 June 1861 the same year as the *Sebastopol* journey states: "The Ship *Montmorency*, after a passage of 105 days from Hong Kong, arrived here on the afternoon of the 27th instant, assigned to Messrs. Jones and Garnet, with 281 Immigrants of whom 17 were females — a fine, contented batch of people. Seven deaths took place on board and one birth. One of the deaths, as we are informed, was from natural causes, and by others from excessive indulgence in the use of opium. The Captain says that he has been in the habit of carrying English, Irish and Scotch to Australia and that he has much more trouble with them than with this last set of immigrants, who were so peaceable and well disposed that he had no occasion to erect a barricade as usual, and they were permitted to walk about the quarter-deck; . . ."[33]

However the *Sebastopol* experienced problems with its Chinese passengers. In the *Royal Gazette* of British Guyana on 1 June 1861 there was the following short article: "When the Ship *Sebastopol* arrived here we had stated that there had been some fighting on board in consequence of an attempt on the part of the immigrants to take possession of the vessel shortly after leaving China, but as we got no particulars furnished to us, and there seemed to be disposition to keep matters quiet, we made . . . allusion to the subject."[35]

It looks as if the mutiny on board was covered up as there are no further details of what happened.

The Demise of the *Sebastopol*

The *Sebastopol* had two journeys to New Zealand with immigrants in 1861 and 1863. After the second journey to New Zealand, the *Sebastopol* sailed from the port of Lyttelton on 22 July 1863, to the port of Callao, Peru.[36]

The *Sebastopol* was going to pick up a cargo of guano for Messrs Thomson & Co. Not a very glamorous cargo but a very important and valuable cargo which would have made the long journey from New Zealand back to Great Britain more economic for the owners of the ship, Kidston & Co.

An interesting article in the North Otago Times, 10 January 1871[37] talks about the guano trade in the 19th century and what the port of Callao was like. A sailing ship took about six weeks to do the journey from Dunedin to Callao. A massive earthquake in 1630 destroyed the city of Callao and land rose, sunk and was split apart in different places. Then there was another earthquake in 1746 which "swallowed up the city of Callao." Callao had improved in condition as a port since the guano trade had brought wealth to the area. The article says "All vessels are obliged to clear here on their arrival and departure. The streets have been widened, the houses improved, and altogether the town looks well from the bay, though it does not bear a close inspection so well, having all the abominations of South American ports."

Numerous vessels crowded the bay. "The harbor generally presents a very lively scene in the number of large and small craft, snuff-colored guano ships, coal ships, steamers, men-of-war, and hundreds of row boats, with white duck awnings, glancing along the placid waters, conveying passengers to and from the shipping."

On one of the Chinchas Islands it was estimated in 1850 that there was a depth of 100 feet of guano on the centre of the island gradually decreasing towards the edges, resting on granite underneath. Its main use was for fertiliser for agriculture. The article discusses the history of the guano trade:

'The Ichaboe or African guano was, it is well-known, introduced through the instigation of Captain Andrew Livingstone of Liverpool, a gentleman well-known in the nautical world. The first cargo sent to England from this coast was from Paquiqui in the *Charles Eyes*, in 1841; and from that period to June, 1858, 2,608,659 tons had been shipped from Peru — a most profitable, readymoney trade for the Peruvian Government, as it took £4 a ton profit. This has become a curious political element. Mr George Peacock reported that in 1846 there were 18,250,000 tons on the Chinchas alone, or about 33,000,000 tons altogether on the coast of Peru. Another estimate gave 250,000,000 tons on the Chinchas alone. At any rate, the quantity was enormous. Since then 24 years have passed, and the islands have been continually yielding. There is considerable waste in shipping the guano, both from tramways and shoots, it being so dry that it blows away in dust. The water was colored out as far as we lay with it. About 1000 sail lay among the islands loading, or waiting for their turn at the shoots. Chinese and native laborers are employed, and much cruelty is practised.'[37]

Chincha guano islands, 1863 (Wikimedia)

The Harbour at Callao, c.1866 (Mánuel A Fuentes)

The *Sebastopol* was another of the many ships that went to pick up a load of guano from the Chincha Islands, to be taken to Cork, Ireland. The ship owners bought an insurance policy with certain limits in the small print. In the course of the voyage the vessel encountered a severe storm going around Cape Horn and put into Rio de Janeiro on 7 February 1864. It was so "damaged by the perils of the sea" that it was not worth repairing and was sold as a wreck on 31 March 1864 at Rio. The cargo of guano was still on board and was stored in a warehouse in Rio de Janeiro. Duncan Taylor procured another vessel, the *Caprice* to carry the guano on to Bristol for an agreed freight of about £2467. There was also a charge of £100 for landing, warehousing and reloading the guano at Rio. The cargo was worth £5003 and was insured for £2000 with Empire Marine Insurance.

The guano arrived safely in England and the owners of the *Sebastopol* were paid the contracted amount. However they were left with costs from storing the guano and sending it by another ship. Kidston and Co. tried to recoup their losses from the Insurance Company based on the "Sue and Labour" clause – that one can claim back reasonable expenses incurred to mitigate a greater loss. The insurance company tried not to pay based on the small print of the policy. The owners of the *Sebastopol* sued and won. The court case,

Kidston & Co. vs. Empire Marine Insurance can still be found in historic English rulings.[8]

So the *Sebastopol* became a casualty of Cape Horn. Cape Horn at the bottom of South America was known as the sailors' graveyard because of the difficultly sailing around it due to large waves, strong winds, large icebergs and strong currents. It was a major milestone on the clipper route as ships had to go around it to deliver trade around the world. When the Panama canal opened in 1914, this made trade easier, but in 1863 this was the only route.[38]

There is no record known of what happened to the *Sebastopol* once it was sold in Rio de Janeiro. Maybe it was repaired and used as a Brazilian ship under the same or a different name. Maybe it was taken apart and turned into something else. But in any case it was the end of the *Sebastopol* as a New Zealand immigrant ship and a British owned and registered vessel.

Ship in stormy seas (Charles Ellms)

The Ship

First Voyage to New Zealand

(5 September 1861 – 14 December 1861)

The First Voyage to New Zealand 1861

In 1861 the *Sebastopol* became a packet ship sailing under the flag of Willis, Gann & Co under engagement by the Canterbury Provincial Government. It set sail from Gravesend near London on 5 September 1861 and arrived in Lyttelton, New Zealand, on 14 December 1861. An advertisement was placed in *The Times* (London, England) on 14 June 1861 for passengers to travel to New Zealand. Many of the steerage passengers had been recruited by Mr Marshman, agent to the Provincial Government.

> NEW ZEALAND.—WILLIS, GANN, and Co.'s LINE.—To follow the Royal Stuart, and under engagement to the Provincial Government.—For CANTERBURY direct, the beautiful full-poop clipper SEBASTOPOL, A 1 at Lloyd's, 992 tons register, 1,800 tons burden, JAMES A. FRASER, Commander; lying in the East India Docks. This magnificent ship has in every respect the usual very superior accommodations of the packets of this line—a handsome poop, commodious house on deck, and lofty 'tween decks well lighted and ventilated. She will carry an experienced surgeon. The Sebastopol has proved herself superior in sailing qualities to some of the finest clippers of the day, is commanded by a gentleman most favourably known in the passenger trade, and will be despatched with strict punctuality. For further particulars apply to Willis, Gann, and Co., No. 3, Crosby Square, E.C.

There is one ship's diary for this journey, written by John McLachlan[39], a bricklayer born in Ardrossan, Ayrshire, Scotland in 1840.[40] John's spelling was very creative and he usually wrote only a line a day, mainly about how fast the boat was travelling and the weather, but there were a few other interesting details about the journey. He never once mentions a passenger by name. He must have become quite good at calculating the longitude and latitude, and recorded them almost daily near the end of the voyage. The following is a summary of the journey from John's diary, with a few added pieces from newspapers.

The *Sebastopol* left the East India Docks on the evening of 4 September 1861 and anchored at Gravesend the next morning. The ship left that night and anchored in the Downs that night. On 7 September they hove anchor. There were a lot of passengers sick. This was probably sea sickness as many of the passengers would have never been at sea before.

In the *Otago Daily Times* 5 December 1861, there was an article stating the ship had left Gravesend, London. It actually left on 5 September, not the 6th as mentioned here.

> The Sebastopol left Gravesend on September 6, with 223 passengers and a large and valuable cargo for Canterbury, New Zealand. A great proportion of her steerage passengers are sent out by Mr. Marshman, the agent for the Provincial Government. She will be followed by the clipper Mystery, to sail punctually on the 15th October.

Engraving of the docks at Gravesend, Kent in 1831
(The Museum of London)

On Sunday 8 September the wind was strong and many of the passengers were still sick. The next day the ship was "beating" about the Isle of Wight and on 12 September they were beating against a head wind not far from the land. There was a strong wind in the Bay of Biscay on 13 September and they had to re-feed the top sails. The next day the wind was still strong and the ship was rolling from side to side, which made many of the passengers sick. On Sunday 15 September the ship pulled clear of the Bay of Biscay, which was often notorious for rough seas,[41] and suddenly the passengers felt healthy again. What a relief it would have been for everyone.

On 19 September it got very hot on board as they headed towards the warmer weather of the Equator and the next day they got a "lite brese" as John wrote it, which happened to be the N.E. trade winds. The day after that a shark came up alongside the boat. John seemed interested by the animals he sighted. After two weeks on the boat the Doctor examined all the passengers on 22 September. In the diary the Doctor always seemed to examine the passengers on the "Sabbath." The passengers saw a few flying fish that afternoon. What a magnificent and unusual sight that would have been for them all.

Sailfin flying-fish (Wikipedia)

On 23 September there was a sick sailor in the hospital, possibly Alexander Souter, who eventually died although no name is given by the diary writer, John. The next day the breeze was light again and the heat was annoying the passengers who were luckily all in good health. On 26 September the wind was strong and variable and the passengers saw a lot of flying fish and dolphins, and on the following day they had their first shower of rain since the journey had started, a heavy shower. On the 29th, another Sunday, the Doctor inspected the passengers. It was dead calm and there was heavy rain.

On the 30th it was calm and rainy and the ship spoke a brig from Newfoundland bound for Rio de Janeiro, laden with fish, in latitude 7° N longitude 29° W.

The first two days of October were calm, sultry and boiling on the decks. On 4 October John wrote a letter home. There were 14 sails in sight, showing how busy the sea was at that part of the ocean in 1861. The next day was, according to John, "calm and rosting [roasting]." On Monday 7 October they could see 18 sails.

They "crossed the Line" (the Equator) at night on 10 October. It sounds like the men were going to shave in celebration of the crossing but a bit of a fight ensued. As John put it, ". . . all preperations was made for shaving but the Captain would not allough it so it passed off quitely with the mate & one of the sailors having a fite."

The ship caught the South East Trades on 11 October and they were travelling at a rate of 7 knots. The weather came in on 16 October and it was blowing very hard, the worst they had seen since they had first set sail. It drove them to within 60 miles of Brazil. John wrote, "We were in Lattituse [latitude] 13 South & 300 miles of [off] our course, we carried away our Spanker & splite our fore tope [top] sail & carried away our main royl [royal]." The storm abated the next day and they were back to normal, much to the relief of everyone.

On Sunday 20 October, they were inspected by the Doctor. They were at latitude 22.18° S. John had to put more clothes on as it was getting very cold. On 23 October it was blowing very hard from the NE. They were running quite fast at about 12 ½ knots.

On 25 October, the young men refused to nurse in the Hospital. According to John, "the Captain threatening to stope [stop] our provisions to a biscuit & water. There is at present 3 fever patients in the Hospital & it is in the young mens compartment & protest to the Dr against it being there." On 26 October, the hospital and patients were moved on deck. The fever was getting very bad.

The following day John wrote, "Cold & Squaly [squally]. The young men had a meeting to take into consideration the propriety of taking a protest against the Captain for not providing Nurses in the Hospital to wait on the sick. We told the Captain we would show it to the Commissioner on landing." The next day they got an answer from the Captain to the effect that he would not provide nurses and the men again protested. There were articles in the paper after landing detailing the men's concerns and the Commissioners didn't think there was a problem, just a lack of human kindness on the part of the men. According to the *Morning Post* of 27 November 1861 the *Sebastopol* was spoken by the *Vision* 22 days out; this would have been about 27 September 1861. The ship was also spoken by the *Nixon*, according to the *Caledonian* Mercury on 26 November 1861. All was well with the *Sebastopol* according to these ships on arrival at Great Britain.

On 30 October the weather was warm and they were at 23.14° S, 14.51° E. The next day John mentioned that it was Halloween and that they were at 36° S, 11.9° E. Whether they had a celebration for Halloween was not mentioned. A few days later on 4 November there was cold sleet and the sick men were recovering. On the 8th John wrote, "We had a meeting to get up a subscription to pay the Nurses in the Hospital."

It was a sad day on 11 November when five month old girl Louisa Dethier died in the morning and was thrown into the deep at 4 o'clock in the afternoon at approximately 46° S, 26° E. They were now in the cold icy waters of the southern Indian Ocean. It was blowing very hard and raining on 12 November and John mentioned that the ship was carrying very little canvas. The next day he thought the ship was at 47.8° S, 31° E, approximately 1000 miles South of South Africa, not far from icebergs.

The ship had a terrible day on 14 November when one of the sailors fell from the mizzen top sail yard, and broke his arm and fractured his skull. He was sitting with the steward and some cabin passengers. We don't know exactly what happened to him after that and no name is mentioned. The sailors decided to go on strike that day as they thought they were not getting enough meat and butter but the Captain got them all on the poop and threatened to starve them out unless they would work. They agreed, having no other alternative. And to make matters worse the sea was coming into the boat during a storm that day and nearly drowned some of the passengers, or as John put it "she shiped a sea & nearly drowned? me & many others. The rain is as cold as ever I felt?"

On 15 November the ship's position was 48.10° S, 40.20° E. At 7 o'clock in the evening they sighted Possession Island (Île de la Possession, Crozet Islands). John McLachlan was the first passenger to see the cold Sub-Antarctic island in the southern Indian Ocean.

One of the Crozet Islands. This is the kind of view that the ship Sebastopol would have had as they passed by in 1861. (Courtesy Wikipedia)

The following day the passengers saw a few sperm whales at 47° S, 54.37° E. On 18 November it was blowing very hard with a heavy sea. John said "In the evening we had the prettiest sunset I ever saw. We were going 9 knots." The following day there was another passenger in the Hospital.

The boat really took off on 28 November. It was blowing very hard and they covered the most miles yet, a total of 304 miles. Their position was 46.40° S, 125.30° E. John didn't mention it in his diary, but, according to his probate, Thomas McFarlane died and his body was thrown into the deep. The ship was travelling 12 to 14 knots on 29 November and it was still blowing very hard from the WNW. This made the ship travel 317 miles in 24 hours. They were positioned at 46.42° S, 135.42° E.

John wrote on 2 December, "Early in the morning it was blowing a gale so much that some of the pass[engers] got out of their beds and rune [run] for the boats. There was a very heavy sea & it rained all day." They were at 48° S, 148° E. On 4 December they were sailing NE with a fine breeze and the ship's position was 46.47° S, 156.8° E.

John said, "On the 2nd? a man died in the Hospital with the fever & was put overbord Imedi[ately?]." No name was mentioned for this passenger. Two days later it was a fine clear morning and they were looking out for land. The wind was WNW and latitude and longitude, 47.41° S, 164.2° E.

On 7 December John said: "We saw an island to the South of New Zealand called The Snares, when we got the wind all ahead. Another of the fever patients died & was put over board immediately. Latitude 48.36 Longitude 168.0." The next day was the Sabbath. John said, "Inspected by the Dr. Wind NE & heavy fog. passengers al low in spirits with Dissapointment." There had been four deaths in total (three mentioned by John) and the previous day had obviously taken its toll on everyone.

The final entry was, "9th. Cold sleet & head wind. Latitude 49.30 Longitude 171.20."

It sounds as if the passengers had endured enough and just wanted to get to dry land and normality. John never wrote about the journey going up the east coast of New Zealand or the arrival at port.

Arrival of the *Sebastopol*

Before the ship *Sebastopol* arrived, there was a report in the *Lyttelton Times* of 11 December 1861 which suggested the *Sebastopol* was going to increase the amount of females in the colony, not just for domestic servant positions, but also as wives for the many men who had already arrived in the colony.

"The great want experienced in the province from the scarcity of female domestic servants will, we hope, be shortly relieved by the arrivals expected per *Sebastopol*. We are advised that there are above thirty single women on board this vessel, and that similar arrivals may be looked for every month during the summer. In the selection of immigrants generally, we believe there is a great difficulty experienced in obtaining the right sort of persons, while there is no lack of applications."

The boat arrived at Lyttelton Harbour, Canterbury, New Zealand on 14 December 1861. The following article was published in the

Lyttelton Times, dated 18 December 1861[42]

"On Saturday afternoon the ship *Sebastopol* arrived in harbour, after a fair passage, which has occupied ninety-nine days from the Downs. She sighted the Snares on the 7th, and has been detained a week beating up the coast. Made a fair passage to the line, but met with light and baffling winds till she got well down south when she made good way till her arrival within sight of the coast. She brings about 186 souls (all ages) on account of the Provincial Government and several other passengers with a moderate amount of cargo, full particulars of which will be found elsewhere. Some sickness occurred when in the tropics and four deaths have taken place during the voyage—three adults and one infant, viz. Thomas McFarlane, aged 19; John Haines, aged 25; Louisa Deth[i]er, aged five months; and a young man named Alexander Souter, not a Government immigrant."

Thomas McFarlane (McFarlin) was originally from Raffrey, County Down, Ireland and Alexander Souter (likely a member of the crew) was from Inverkeithney, Turriff, Banffshire, Scotland.[43] The infant girl who died Louisa Dethier was daughter of Theodore and Jane Dethier (née Wood). On a more positive note, they had another daughter in Christchurch born the next year on 4 October 1862, named Emily Louisa Dethier; her middle name was after her deceased sister.[44]

The ship discharged its cargo and then sailed for Moulmein (Mawlamyine), Burma (Myanmar) on 16 January 1862. What they were picking up at this port is unknown. The ship would have eventually returned to Great Britain for the next load of emigrants to come to New Zealand.

First Voyage to New Zealand

Map of the Journey of the *Sebastopol*

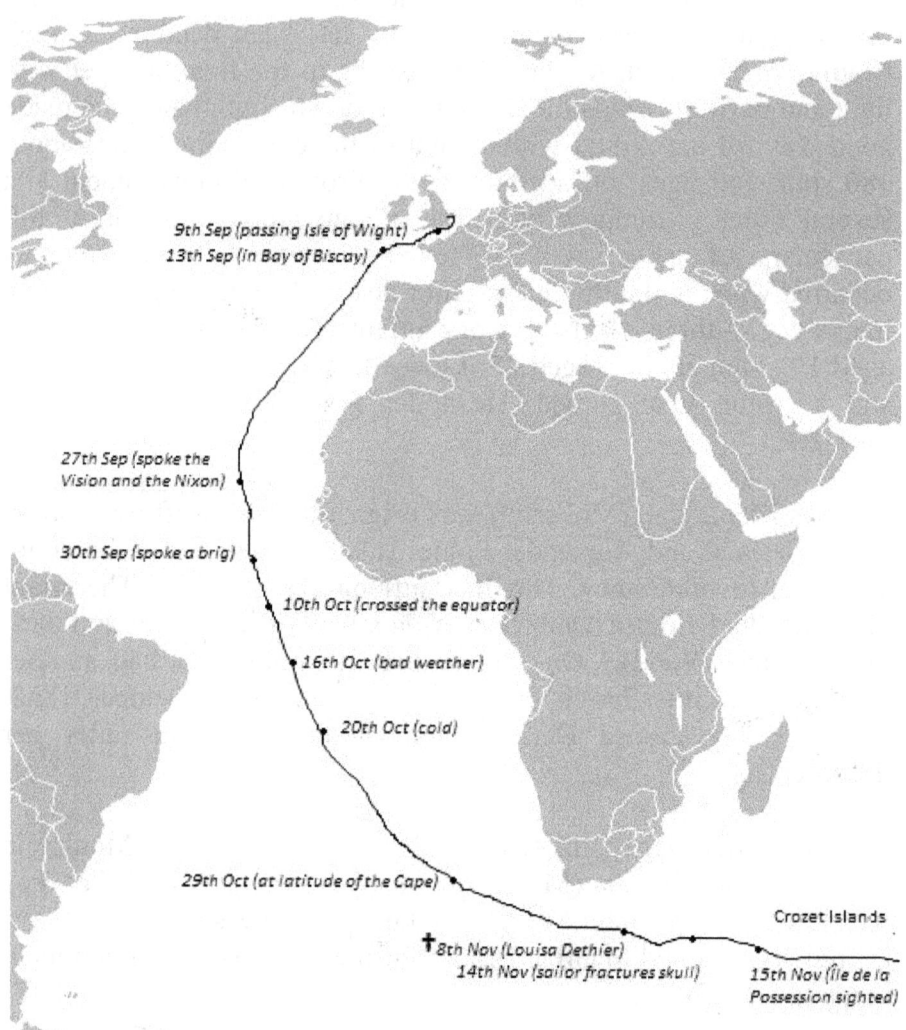

(5 September 1861 – 14 December 1861)

Possessions of an Immigrant

Thomas McFarlane (sometimes spelt McFarlin) died on board the ship *Sebastopol* aged 19. He had with him two trunks of possessions that arrived in Lyttelton after he had been buried at sea. There was a probate for him where James Archibald Fraser, Master of the ship, had to state that Thomas was a passenger on board from the North of Ireland and that he had died on or about the 28 November 1861. There was also an inventory of items that the dead man owned; they were not worth more than £50. This reads as an interesting list of the possessions of an immigrant. It is a sad list to read. The items were auctioned off at Lyttelton for £19 12s 3d to pay for the lawyer, but the books worth 7s 9d and £14 cash were sent back to his father, Hugh McFarlin, in Ireland.[45]

> One watch
> One chain
> Pilot Coat
> Bed Tick
> Clothes Bag
> 2 Pair Trousers
> Coat and vest
> 2 Jackets
> 14 pair socks and worsted to mend
> 2 pair boots
> 10 shirts and one shirt
> Coat and waistcoat
> Flannel drawers
> 3 Scarfs
> 5 Handkerchiefs
> 2 Cups
> 1 Pr Hose
> 1 Quilt
> 1 Towel
> 1 Brush
> 1 Box of collars and sundries
> 2 Chests and sundries in one
> Bible Catechism Hymn Book
> Testament and a Likeness

Sebastopol Cargo 1861

IMPORTS.

In the Sebastopol, Dalgety and Co., agents; 45 barrels, 4 tierces, 486 cases, 28 bales, 123 casks, 39 qr-casks, 100 boxes, 2 crates, 4 octaves, 1 basket, 41 pkgs. machinery, 5 hhds, 6 sheets lead, 30 drums oil, 15 do. turpentine, 10 bundles, 300 bags salt, 30 hhds ale, 50 cases bottled stout, 50 do. ale, 125 casks bottled beer, 6 anvils, 6 pair bellows, 6 forge irons, 41 tons iron, 148 bags, 60 tons coals, Dalgety and Co.; 60 drums oil, 4 cases, 1 bale, 2 hhds., W. Wilson; 5 hhds. wine, 7 casks 10 qr-casks, Hargreaves; 41 cases, 18 iron axles, 45 bundles, 4 trusses rope, 29 bars, 34 plates iron, 4 pkgs. reapers, 7 casks 5 hhds. 2 pair bellows, 1 cask zinc, 6 sheets lead, 17 kegs nails, 1 pkge. agricultural implements, 12 bales iron buckets, 1 pipe oil, 13 anvils, 1 truss cordage, 2 boxes, E. Reece and Co.; 14 hhds., 3 cases, 250 casks bottled beer, 15 pkgs., 80 casks, Cookson and Co.; 14 casks wine, 12 hhds. ale, 4 pkgs. machinery, 15 bundles, 1 crate, 5 cases, 39 kegs., 10 casks, 4 hhds., Hawkes and Stroutes; 4 qr-casks wine, 30 cases, 120 boxes, 5 bundles, 4 bags, 4 casks, 4 qr-casks, 3 hhds., 22 brrels, 61 kegs, 10 firkins, 6 drums, 7 crates, 308 sash weights, 3 half-tierces tobacco, 10 weights, 12 bundles buckets, Order; 3 chests, 10 cases, 2 boxes, 2 trunks, 18 pkgs. house, 12 bundles planks, W. Poyndestre; 106 casks bottled beer, 72 pkgs., 1 parcel samples, Heywood and Co.; 3 pkgs. agricultural implements, H. Moore; 1 case Leigh, 13 pkgs. drapery, 1 case, B. Ware; 1 case looking glasses, 2 cases, Burnell and Bennett; 1 pkge apparel, Miss Andrews, 1 do., Porter; 1 case dresses, Whitcombe; 1 box, Veel; 1 case Tripe; 1 do. C. Davie; 1 box books, C. H. Brown; 2 cases clothing, R. Roberts; 4 pkgs. F. Strouts; 1 case, E. Mallinson; 5 do., S. Johnson; 3 boxes, J. Bates; 2 cases, H. Dunsford; 8 pkgs. agricultural implements, Davies; 4 pkgs. dog-carts, Miles and Co.; 1 case books, King; 400 bars iron, 58 bundles do., H. Kite; 1 box apparel, J. F. Peel; 1 case tools; G. Thomas; 1 box irons, 1 case agricultural implements, Hodgson; 1 case H. Laing; 4 trunks boots, Goodman; 2 cases Edmiston; 8 pkgs., Dr. Fisher; 2 cases, Butler; 1 case piano, 1 do. ploughs, Kennaway, 10 bales stationery, Ward and Reeves; 1 case, J. Williams; 4 pkgs. carts, J. King; 1 case, 2 cases perfumery, 10 cases wine, 3 cases madeira, Order; 1 case, Hall; 1 case, H. Torlesse; 5 cases furniture, E. Butler; 10 drums oil, Bain; 10 pkgs., A. Matthews; 4 pkgs. machinery, J. Miln; 2 cases clocks, C. Asmussen; 1 case, F. Jollie; 2 bundles, Snead; 17 pkgs., Pilbrow; 1 pkgs. bowls, H. Hanmer; 33 pkgs., Neeve; 493 pkgs. iron standards, Gould and Miles; 1 hhd. spirits-wine, Turnbull and Hillson; 1 case apparel, S. Bealey; 1 .box, Robinson; 1 pkge., Lock; 1 case apparel, J. Morgan; 1 case, boots, Fysh; 1 case apparel, Grinders; 2 pkgs., Bartrum; 1 case haberdashery, Mrs. Williams; 1 box apparel, G. A. Reade; 1 piano, F. J. Moss.

List of cargo on board the Sebastopol, Press, 21 December 1861

Provincial Secretary's Office,
Christchurch, Dec. 20, 1861.

HIS Honor the Superintendent directs the publication of the following report of the Immigration Commissioners on the ship Sebastopol for general information:—

SHIP SEBASTOPOL.

The commissioners report that they found the ship well ordered, the provisions of good quality, they heard no complaints of any kind, excepting from the single men, who handed the document appended.

The commissioners have made enquiries into the several matters referred to. The principal dissatisfaction appears to have arisen from the young men being called upon to undertake the duties of nursing one of their messmates. In this the commissioners consider that the surgeon-superintendent exercised a wise discretion in a matter not clearly provided for in the regulations, and that the recusant passengers evinced not only insubordination, but want of natural kindness.

The commissioners recommend that, to prevent a similar misunderstanding in future ships, a distinct provision for appointing and remunerating extra nurses be made in the published regulations.

The difficulty in the cooking department appears to have been caused by the act of the passengers themselves in neglecting to comply with the instructions of the captain and surgeon in the regulation of the messes.

The commissioners recommend that more care be taken in placing the galley in immigrant vessels.

The insinuations against the accuracy of the weights appear wholly unsupported by facts.

The commissioners are assured that the surgeon's visits were regular and that he passed hours daily in the 'tween decks.

The commissioners consider that a grave error was committed in placing a seaman affected with fever in the immigrants' hospital. They do not however believe that the fever was continued by contagion. As far as they can now ascertain, the four cases were produced by the men sleeping on the open deck by day and night in spite of the remonstrances of the authorities.

Signed,
WILLIAM DONALD, CHAIRMAN.
H. S. McKELLAR, } Commissioners
WM. REEVES, } of
JOHN T. ROUSE, } Immigration.

Lyttelton, December 18, 1861.

Lyttelton Times, 21 December 1861

MRS. LEWIS, an experienced MONTHLY NURSE, who arrived by the Sebastopol, is desirous of an engagement. Address Mrs. Lewis, at Mrs. Paddy's, Montreal street, south, Christchurch. 284

Lyttelton Times, 11 January 1862

Passengers on the 1861 Voyage

Passengers on the 1861 Voyage

Brough

William Brough settled in Springburn, inland from Ashburton, Canterbury. In 1869 he entered the Ellesmere Ploughing Match and was awarded a pair of blinkers as a prize for the best team on the ground.[46] His wife, Mary Stuart Brough, died in 1892 aged 68. William Brough died in 1907 aged 79.[47] They are buried in Ashburton Cemetery.[48]

Cassin

Michael Cassin was a maltster (a maker of malt) who at one stage lived at Pigeon Lane, Addington, Christchurch. He married Mary Lawlor (Lallor) in 1862. In 1900 a Michael Cassin was fined 10s for larrikinism after drinking too much and damaging a glass door at the Heathcote Hotel, along with William Cassin.[49] Michael died in 1917 and is buried in Sydenham Cemetery, Christchurch.[50]

Eckhoff

Henry Eckhoff and his wife Wilhelmina were mentioned in the Star 6 October 1879. Henry appears to have been a violent man and needed to learn to keep the "heck off" his poor wife.[51]

> VIOLENT ASSAULT—Henry Eckhoff was charged with having violently assaulted Wilhelmina Eckhoff, his wife, on Oct. 4. On the case being called on, Sergeant Morice stated that the accused had assaulted his wife on the previous Saturday, by striking her with a bottle and cutting her head open. The woman would probably have to remain in the Hospital four or five days, and a remand for a week was desired, the accused to be brought up sooner if necessary. Sergeant Morice added that the woman did not desire to prosecute, but that the police would offer evidence. The adjournment was granted, and subsequently, on the application of Mr Neck, His Worship decided to allow bail, one good surety in the sum of £50, or two sureties in the sum of £25 each.

Fabling

William Fabling was born in Kent, England but lived in Peckham Rye, London before leaving on the *Sebastopol*. He worked for Joseph Brittan for many years and in 1873 left Christchurch and bought a farm at Brookside, Canterbury. Five years before his death he moved to Leeston. He married twice. The first marriage produced children. *Ellesmere Guardian*, printed an obituary for William Fabling which said "Mr Fabling was naturally of a quiet, reserved disposition, but was always recognised as an upright, conscientious man, and his death will cause a large circle of friends to mourn." He died in 1899.[52]

Greig

John Greig was born in Ross-shire, Scotland in 1839 and worked on farms for the Duke of Leeds, the Mitchells of Linfearn and Messrs Tait and Urquhart of Strathglass. He married Christina McIntosh of Glenurquhart, Inverness-shire in 1861 before travelling to New Zealand on the *Sebastopol*. He worked for Messrs Kennaway, Lee and Acton, of Opawa station, Timaru, and was afterwards with Mr. Sheath, of Birmingham. He then became a farmer at Pleasant Point, where he was closely involved in the community. He was a member of the Pleasant Point school committee for a number of years, and was chairman of the cemetery board and library committee. John and Christina had five sons and two daughters.[53]

Mr & Mrs Greig

Hickey

Cornelius Hickey, from Cork, Ireland, was a farmer at Addington, Christchurch. He married Mary Murphy in 1864. Cornelius was fined numerous times for letting cattle roam in the streets of Christchurch.[54] He died in 1888. His wife Mary died at Harman Street, Addington in 1900.[55] She was a devout Catholic and at her death their grown up family consisted of one son and five daughters.[56] Cornelius and Mary's daughters Norah and Margaret had weddings on the same day at the Catholic Cathedral in Christchurch on 24 April 1907.[57]

Hunter

Robert Hunter and his wife Barbara (née Farnley) travelled from Aberdeenshire, Scotland. They had two children, Georgina born in 1850 who must have died before they came to New Zealand and Elizabeth Hunter baptised 1852 at Inverurie who travelled on the ship *Sebastopol* with her parents. After arriving in New Zealand, Robert became a carter and the family lived at Peraki Street, Kaiapoi. Robert died in 1882 in Kaiapoi and is buried at St Bartholomew's Cemetery, Kaiapoi. Barbara died in 1898 and is buried at Addington Cemetery, Christchurch.

Kerr

Edward George Kerr was born in 1845 in Glasgow, Scotland. After arriving in New Zealand aged 16, he became a storekeeper at Kaiapoi for a few years.

Edward spent ten years on the staff of the *Lyttelton Times* as an agent and correspondent for North Canterbury. He moved to South Canterbury in 1877 where he tried to extend the circulation of the paper. He then moved to North Otago where he was agent and correspondent for the area until 1881. The same year he bought the *South Canterbury Times* which he ran for seven years before buying the *Timaru Herald* in 1887. He ran the two papers at the same time for twelve years. In 1901 he concentrated on the Herald.

Edward was the Mayor of Kaiapoi for five years (1872-1876) and was associated with many boards and organisations in the Kaiapoi area. He owned a property of 650 acres called *Harlan* in Kingsdown, Otago, where he grew grain and kept sheep. He married Miss Goldthorpe, who was from Cheshire, England, and they had four sons and six daughters.[58]

Ligget

Robert Ligget was born in 1838 in County Armagh, Ireland. He spent his early years on his father's farm. After arriving in New Zealand with his wife Mary, he worked for the Rev. John Raven for a few years before purchasing a farm in Waikuku, North Canterbury. He added to his farm over the years and called it *Tullyhue*.[59] Robert and Mary Ligget had many children. Robert died on 21 December 1918 at Waikuku.[60]

Mr R. Ligget

Lord

William Lord, married Ellen Chisman on 24 August 1861 at Bradford, Yorkshire and William sailed aged 20 aboard the *Sebastopol* to New Zealand. Jabez Lord, William's brother, and Thomas Milner sponsored William to New Zealand. William's wife, Ellen, arrived 29 January 1863 on the *Chariot of Fame*, sponsored by her husband. William and Ellen had eleven children, six sons and five daughters. Tom and Charles were born in Christchurch and the rest of the children born in Taradale, west of Napier. Two of the children had short lives and are buried in Napier Cemetery. William was a grocer in Christchurch and a ploughman and well sinker in Taradale. Ellen died at Taradale on 08 September 1909 and is buried with her two young daughters at Napier Public Cemetery. William died at Hastings on 01 May 1922 and is buried at Hastings.[61]

Mr W. Lord & son William

May

George May was born in Bristol, England, in 1830. In his younger years he was in the Royal Navy in the Mediterranean, during Garibaldi's war. He also joined a Chilean man-of-war, and was present at some engagements between the Chilean and Peruvian troops. He lived for six years in America before travelling to New Zealand in 1861. He settled in Balcairn, North Canterbury, where he owned a number of properties. He worked as a painter, painter, sailmaker, sawyer, bridge builder and farmer. At age seventy three he was still strong and hearty and could still carry a full bag of wheat.[62]

McLachlan

John McLachlan was born in Ardrossan, Ayrshire, Scotland, in 1840. John's diary is the only known ship's diary for the ship *Sebastopol*. His trade was plasterer and after arriving in New Zealand he explored the country a bit before deciding to settle on land near Lake Ellesmere where he became a farmer. McLachlan represented the Ashburton electorate in the New Zealand House of Representatives for twelve years from 1893-1896 and from 1899-1908. He was apparently a colourful character in Parliament.

John McLachlan c. 1900

"The representative of Ashburton", wrote a newspaper reporter, "is about the wildest looking specimen in the Parliamentary collection. But if he is in the rough to gaze on, he can give 'points' to some more ornamental members in the matter of ability and originality of thought and expression. He is a sturdily built, carelessly dressed man, with a large head, made to look larger by the wild disorder of a huge shock of curly hair. He is a farmer and might have stepped out of his market trap into his place in the House. He is, as a rule, a breezy, happy-go-lucky sort of member with a good sense of humour and a fine stock of anecdotes and a great admiration for and acquaintance with the writings of Robert Burns."

He loved his whisky and occasionally made a fool of himself while speaking in parliament. In 1894 he fell into the Wellington Harbour while drunk but survived the ordeal. John McLachlan died in 1915.[40]

Moorhead

Michael Moorhead was born about 1835 in County Down, Ireland. He took up land at Southbridge after arriving in Canterbury in 1861. He married and after he died in 1899 left one son and six daughters. According to *The Star* 19 July 1899 Page 4, he was "much respected in the Ellesmere district" and his funeral was "largely attended."

Power

John Power and his brother Michael Power (with wife Mary and infant son John) left Carrickbeg County, Waterford, Ireland in 1861 on the *Sebastopol*, following other family members who had travelled in the 1850s to New Zealand. They brought with them Barbara Power, John and Michael's mother, who was described as a widow and housekeeper. John worked with the Rhodes brothers at Purau, then known as Rhodes Bay. He was probably also a sawyer at Church Bush, Flaxton. Michael and his wife Mary also worked at Purau for the Rhodes Brothers.

In 1863 John purchased 50 acres of land which is now on Lineside Road, Flaxton and made it farmable, taking away the scrub and bush remnants. In 1867 he married Jane Lynskey of Kaiapoi, who was also from Ireland.

Michael and Mary moved to Ohoka and ran a cheese factory and later a farm. John and his family moved to Hawarden where he became well respected and established. Michael died in 1892 aged 52 and Mary took her life six months later.

John fathered ten children and Michael fathered nine.[63]

Rainey

Robert Rainey was born in County Antrim, Ireland in 1841. His early life was spent on his father's farm. Robert married Mary Wallace of Rasharkin, County Antrim, Ireland, in 1861. He farmed at Ferry Road for quite a few years before moving to Lincoln Lodge, Lincoln where he farmed over 300 acres. He engaged in dairy farming and then grew grain and root crops. He bred Clydesdale horses and won many prizes at shows. He bred Shorthorn cattle of a milking strain, which were first favourites at Lincoln Lodge and Tai Tapu. He was one of the main promoters of the Tai Tapu Dairy Factory and was chairman of the company. He was a Justice of the Peace and a member of many local committees and boards. Robert and Mary had two sons and five daughters.[64]

Mr. R. Rainey

Sandrey

George Sandrey was born in Bude, Cornwall, England in 1843 and learnt agriculture on his father's farm in Devonshire. He arrived in New Zealand in 1861 on the *Sebastopol* and took up a job carting supplies from the wharf at Woolston to Christchurch. Eighteen months later he became a partner for three years in a carting firm called Barrett, Comer and Co. In 1865 he started farming on Lincoln Road and five years later bought land at Leeston. He did a lot of road contracting in the area and also had a carrying business between Southbridge and Christchurch before the railway started up. He had a five horse wagon that travelled twice weekly between the two places. He was heavily involved in the affairs of the local district. He bred draught entires and introduced the first draught entires in the Ellesmere

Mr. G. Sandrey

District. In 1896 George moved to Carberry Farm, Weedons which was about 100 acres of freehold land and 300 acres of leasehold land. At the same time he also owned another freehold farm of 600 acres at West Melton. He was on the Courtenay Road Board and belonged to the Lodge Ionic at Leeston. In 1865 he married Harriet Blackler, daughter of James Blackler who arrived on the ship Canterbury in 1851. George and Harriet had six sons and two daughters. [65]

Shewry

Thomas Shewry only lasted a few months in New Zealand before drowning, as reported by the Lyttelton Times 5 March 1862.

> DEATH FROM DROWNING.—Yesterday, an inquest was held at the Resident Magistrate's Court, Lyttelton, before the Coroner, W. Donald, Esq., and a respectable jury, of whom Mr. Willcox was foreman, to enquire into the circumstances touching the death of Thomas Shewry, aged 37, whose body was found floating in the water near Dampiers Bay, early the same morning. It appeared from the evidence that the deceased, who had lately commenced business in Lyttelton as a merchant, having arrived from England in the Sebastopol, had been unwell for some time, and was then suffering in his mind from the effects of intemperate habits. On the night previous to his decease, he was staying at Gosnell's boarding house, and is supposed, at about 4 a.m., to have dropped from the window of his bedroom and gone down to the seaside. The jury gave a verdict of "Found drowned, the deceased having been of unsound mind since the 28th of February, but how he got into the water there was no evidence to show."

Willes

William Aubrey Willes was born in England in 1839. He was known as Willie Willes and Canterbury aged 22 in the *Sebastopol* as a Chief Cabin passenger. He went into partnership with Henry de Bourbel, as corn & flour merchants and general commission agents. They did well in the 1860s. Willie travelled back to England in 1864 to research and purchase a steam driven plough for the Sefton Farmers' Club. The trip was successful, and the machine and traction engine arrived on the ship *David Brown* in 1866. Willes lived at a property named *Ravenswood* in Woodend until the early 1870s when he moved to Waipara Flats, North Canterbury. Willie inherited a 2000 acre property from Arthur Powys. Willie named the property Astrop after his old home in Northamptonshire, England.[66]

Zuppicich

Antonio Zosef Zuppicich was born in Austria in 1841 and was brought up to a seafaring life. He travelled to NZ on the *Sebastopol*, but is not on the passenger list. He may have been a crew member but we don't have a record to prove this. He lived for a short time in Timaru before settling at Woodend, North Canterbury in 1862 where he became a farmer. He married in 1863 to Mary Ann Cleaver, daughter of Henry Cleaver of Woodend who came out on the *Cressy*, one of the first four ships to Canterbury. Antonio and Mary Ann had three sons and four daughters. He died in 1908 in Kaiapoi.[67]

The Second Voyage to New Zealand

(17 January 1863 – 21 May 1863)

The Second Voyage to New Zealand 1863

The *Sebastopol* departed Gravesend, London, on 17 January 1863 and arrived at Lyttelton, New Zealand, on 21 May 1863 under the command of Captain Duncan Taylor.

There are no known ship diaries for this voyage, but it could be seen as a voyage without too many trials. All ships to New Zealand at this time took the same route around the bottom of Africa and Australia, catching the "roaring forties" which took them at a fast pace to their destination. There were no deaths on board, a very rare thing, suggesting top class management of the vessel.

There was a suggestion that Willis, Gann & Co. had made Captain Duncan Taylor's job hard with their "illiberal arrangements", putting many obstacles in his way. There is no suggestion as to what these obstacles were. Captain Taylor ensured that the passengers had every comfort.[68]

The worst part of the journey was the bad weather in the early part of the journey which caused slow progress. The passengers would have likely experienced extreme sea sickness at this time, until they cleared Great Britain and came out of the bad weather. The sickness would have made many fearful of what was to come. The German passengers had already had a rough journey over the North Sea to get to London. Many passengers would have been beside themselves with worry that the whole journey would be bad. But it was only the first three weeks that proved very bad, weather wise. Captain Duncan Taylor spent many nights checking on the passengers at the expense of his own sleep, suggesting much unrest of the passengers.[68] After the journey, the passengers spoke highly of Captain Taylor, surgeon Dr Galbraith and the officers. Just before the ship arrived in port the passengers presented the men with testimonials and the Captain received a purse of sovereigns and an address which had 230 signatures.

On 4 February the *Sebastopol* was off the Needles,[69] which is a series of three stacks of chalk which are at the western extremity of the Isle of Wight. The passengers and crew would have also sighted the Needles Lighthouse, built in 1859.[70]

Heavy gales continued for a long time and the ship was finally clear of Great Britain on 9 February.

There were some passengers on this journey who were not named on the passenger list. This can be easily seen when adding up the list and comparing it to newspaper reports which said that there were 205 assisted Government emigrants. On the passenger list are about 187 assisted passenger names. The Captain Duncan Taylor received an address containing 230 signatures from his passengers, including his crew which would have numbered about 40. One of the third mates was George Glegg Gardner from Deal, Kent. He was on the ship on its return journey to England. He would have experienced the terrible storms around Cape Horn and helped Captain Taylor get the ship into Rio de Janeiro, where it ended its life as an immigrant ship.[71]

(The Needles from Isaac Taylor's "one inch map" of Hampshire, published in 1759, showing "Lot's Wife," the needle-shaped pillar that collapsed in a storm in 1764, Courtesy Wikipedia)

There were many Irish passengers on board, along with a large amount of Germans for one voyage. Imagine the different accents and languages all mixed together; Irish, Scottish, English and German all talking at once in the saloon.

A letter to *Sebastopol* passenger Karl Philipp Meng from his family in Hohen-Sülzen, Germany sent in 1863, commented that they had waited half a year to hear from him and were very worried. "We at home trembled and you danced and had concerts."[72] Passenger Karl Friedrich Zinckgraf was a fine pianist and also ran a choir in his home town of Kindenheim, Germany, so would have been sought after for his musical talents in entertaining the passengers. Pianos were often in the saloons of immigrant ships. One can just imagine Mr Zinckgraf playing the piano, people singing and dancing; men drinking and staggering about the ship, swirling the women around in large skirts. The children would have been trying to sleep in the family quarters. It would have been raucous, the smell of booze and sweat filling the air!

The third mate George Glegg Gardner was charming the young dairymaid Margaret McKinley until they were virtually engaged by the end of the voyage.[71] They probably danced at every chance they could get.

The Ship's Surgeon, and chronic alcoholic, Charles John Galbraith would have been sitting in his cabin away from everyone, drinking too much and becoming intoxicated. Jane Jameson's cabin was next to the Surgeon's cabin and she could hear him through the wall. At dinner he would be sitting on a bench in the saloon wallowing in his sorrows while others were socialising around him. Occasionally he would talk to passengers about his woes. He had insomnia from depression and also stomach complaints.[73]

On 9 March, 49 days out, they spoke the ship *Howden*, from Bombay to Liverpool; on 7 March, ship *Ocean Mail*, from London to Shanghai; on 20 March, ship *New Era*, from London to Madras.[74]

During the day they would have walked on deck, noticing land in the distance, dark lumps some distance off, islands, continents. Some stretches of the journey there would have been sea all around with no land visible. They would have seen dolphins jumping, possibly whales, flying fish and other amazing creatures. The sails of many other ships would have been noticed in the busy shipping areas of the Atlantic Ocean and then it would have seemed extremely lonely as they rounded the Cape of Good Hope at the bottom of Africa into the southern Indian Ocean; very few ships, only a couple of mysterious islands and maybe the odd iceberg and just vast ocean around them. The Southern Cross would have been visible in the sky at night and they would have all been talking of their new land.

Mr Philip Tisch and Mr H.C.H. Knowles, who had already lived in New Zealand for a while and were making a return trip after visits home, would have likely done lectures and talks on the country and where the best places to settle were, and what their experiences were.

There was a marriage and three births on board the *Sebastopol* but these were not listed in the passenger lists after arrival, or in the newspapers. Only one of the births is known; that of a baby girl.

Assisted emigrant Elizabeth Baxter was pregnant when she boarded the ship *Sebastopol*. She was in confinement for a month on board the ship after the birth of her daughter Elizabeth Ann Baxter on 25 April 1863 while still at sea.[44] While on board there was a terrible accident and one of her children was scalded. We don't know how many children she had as her family was not listed on the passenger list. Elizabeth must have been under huge stress and had what was described in the newspaper as an epileptic fit. She then became extremely weak. She had not handled her child's accident well and had just endured a birth at sea. On arrival in New Zealand she was taken to the hospital. She had something to eat at Sumner but died shortly after, on 27 May, in the hospital, from what the coroner described as "Died by the Visitation of God".[75] She was buried on 28 May 1863 at Barbadoes St Cemetery. Sadly her husband John Baxter, named as a farm bailiff, died only a month later and was buried on 29 June 1863 next to his wife, leaving Elizabeth Ann a 2 month old orphan. The tiny baby Elizabeth Ann never had her birth registered in New Zealand. She was received into the Church (which means she had already been baptised previously, either on the ship or in Christchurch) on 21 Sept 1864 and sponsors were the Venerable Henry Jacobs, and his wife, Charlotte Emily Jacobs, of St Michael and All Angels, as well as an Anne Laraman, (we don't know her relationship to the child).[44] There is no mention of the other children in the records. One can only hope that the orphaned children went on to live happy lives in their new country.

On 19 May 1863, the *Sebastopol* spoke the U.S. whaling ship *Illinois*, 43 months out, carrying 2300 barrels oil.[76] This ship was off the coast of New Zealand where whaling ships plundered the ocean's riches until there were hardly any whales left.

The *Sebastopol* arrived in the port of Lyttelton on 21 May 1863 at about 5pm.

Map of the Journey of the *Sebastopol* 1863

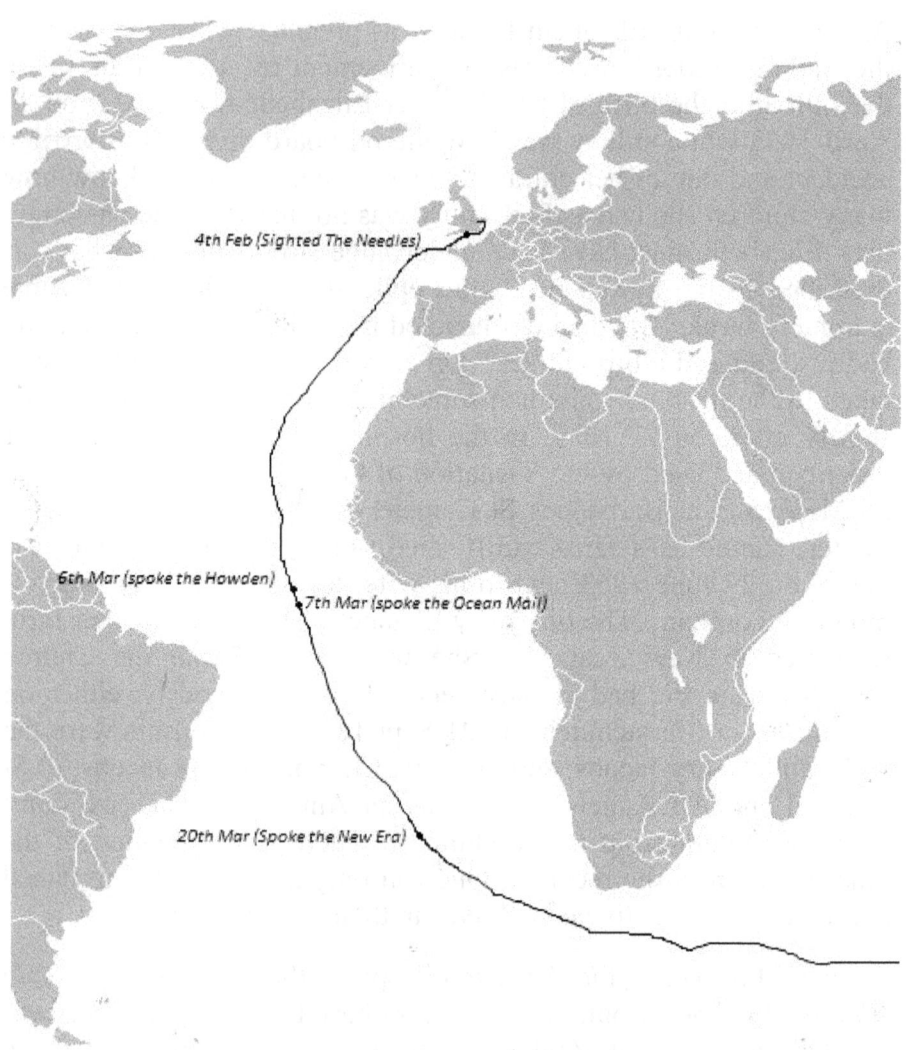

(17 January 1863 – 21 May 1863)

The Second Voyage to New Zealand

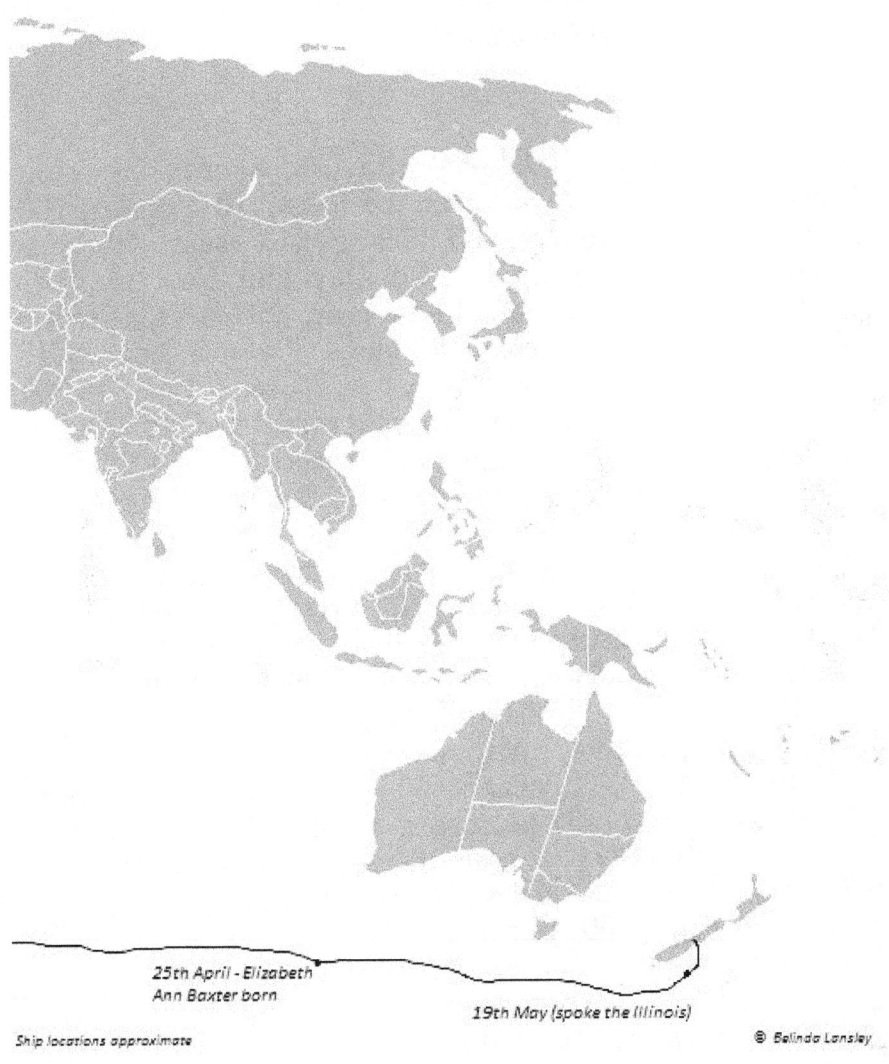

Sebastopol Cargo 1863

The Lyttelton Municipal Council was expecting the municipal seal to arrive on the *Sebastopol*, after information from Mr Marshman, agent for the Provincial Government.[77]

Other cargo included:

> In the Sebastopol, Dalgety and Co., agents: 5 cases, 32 casks, 30 drums, 20 bundles, 28 cases, 10 bundles, 100 boxes, 3 cases, 25 bundles, 33 packages, 3 cases, 40 hhds ale, 200 cases ditto, Dalgety, Buckley and Co.; 25 hhds ale, Heywood and Co.; 24 hhds beer, 79 cases, Hawkes and Strouts; 1 case, 4 pkgs, 35 cases, 7 cases, 3 cases, 18 drums, 46 casks, 1 case, 176 pkgs, 27 coils rope, Order; 2 cases merchandise, 22 bars iron, 34 bundles ditto, Anderson; 5 cases, 1 case, Buller; 11 cases order, 4 hhds, 2 casks, 2 casks, Hargreaves; 6 casks, 2 hhds, 7 qr.-casks, R. Waitt; 2 tierces, Rowley; 2 cases, Stringer; 1 case, Butters; 1 cask seeds, Ivory; 4 trunks boots, Order; 1 box, Creyke; 1 case, Roberts, 1 box, Locke; 1 box, Stout; 1 case, Milne; 2 bundles, cart and 2 wheels, Tomkins; 1 case, Day; 48 bars, 108 plates, 18 bundles iron, 101 packages, Reece and Co.; 1 case, Build; 1 case, Read; 16 qr.-casks, Mr. Justice Gresson; 5 pkgs, M'Kellar; 7 cases, Heyward; 50 hhds beer, Strangmoor; 60 drums, Wilson; 33 packages, Bealey; 1 case, Milton; 1 case, Studholme; 1 case, Strout; 10 cases, Merson; 540 cases, Gould and Miles; 1 case, Bonnington; 20 qr.-casks, Peacock; 50 pkgs, 16 ditto, 1 pillar ironwork, Woodgate and Co.; 6 cases, 6 hhds, Booth; 1 box, Sippit; 13 cases, L. E. Nathan; 1 case, Donald; 2 cases, Bushell; 8 cases, Malzon; 2 cases, Wilson; 8 pkgs, Samson; 441 packages, 1200 slates, Stanley; 1 box seeds, Miles and Co.; 6 qr.-casks, 75 cases, box samples, Cookson, Bowler and Co.; 1 case, D. Clarkson; 6 case, Provincial Secretary.

List of Cargo on the Sebastopol, *Lyttelton Times* 23 May 1863

The German Passengers

There were many English, Scottish and Irish migrants on board when the *Sebastopol* travelled in 1863, but also approximately 34 Germans, possibly more. It is important to state that Germany (Deutsches Reich) itself didn't exist until 1871, after the war against the French was won, but in this book the migrants will be called Germans for ease of reference.

A lot of Germans immigrated to America but this group went to New Zealand encouraged by cheaper passage to New Zealand due to Provincial Government paying part of the fare, and the wonderful stories of Mr Philipp Tisch. Philipp immigrated to New Zealand in 1851 aboard the *Midlothian* and had returned to Germany after the death of his father in 1862. He sailed back to Germany with his wife and at least three children aboard the *Mermaid*, leaving from Lyttelton on 2 May 1862.[78] Philipp stayed in the village of Kindenheim, where his mother still lived. Whilst there, Philipp told many wonderful stories of New Zealand. The villagers all listened and thought conditions sounded much better in New Zealand than where they were living. Philipp was also acting as an agent for the Canterbury Provincial Government, so there was a financial incentive for him.

The main reason for German emigration at this time can be summarised by one word - poverty. After 1814 the people of Kindenheim (which is currently in Rheinland-Pfalz) were living in the Kingdom of Bavaria (Königreich Bayern). A few miles away was the border with the next German state, the Grand Duchy of Hassia (Großherzogtum Hessen), which included the village of Hohen-Sülzen where *Sebastopol* passenger Karl Meng lived. The frontier between the two German states was between the villages of Hohen-Sülzen and Bockenheim, and between Offstein and Bockenheim. KB (Königreich Bayern) was written on one side of the frontier stones, on the other side GH (Großherzogtum Hessen). The Germans made a joke of the stones saying KB stood for Kein Brot (no bread) and GH for Großer Hunger (big hunger). Families often had eight or more children and land was split between family members every generation, so land parcels got smaller and smaller, leaving little land on which to grow crops and survive. There were also low prices for crops at this time and in 1857 a drought meant less food was produced. From family stories collected for this book, it seems some young men also wanted to avoid compulsory army service; although this was probably a less important reason for emigration.

Philipp Tisch and emigrants from the village of Kindenheim and surrounding villages travelled together on the *Sebastopol*. One of the passengers was schoolmaster Karl Friederich Zinckgraf who sent letters back to his home village. These letters were published in Germany in 1910. The first letter describes the journey from Kindenheim following the Rhine to the Netherlands, then sailing over the Channel to London, England to board the *Sebastopol,* and the trials and tribulations of the Germans. This was a great adventure for them and they were rejoicing at the prospect of a better life.

"London, 14th January 1863

Dear friends!

The reason that I write these lines is to tell you how it was on our journey and here [in London]. In Mainz we stayed overnight (5 January) and had a nice evening together, then went on board to sleep and left Tuesday (6 January) for Cologne, where we had another lovely evening. Wednesday we went to Emmerich / Bobarth, where they wanted to check our passports and our luggage, but because of a list I had written with the help of the driver, it luckily didn't happen.

In Nymwegen we stayed another night (7 January) and arrived in Rotterdam the next day at 12 o'clock at lunchtime. There we stayed with Brehm in the hotel Bayrischer Hof until Saturday (10 January), where the ship to London was leaving at 1 pm.

Brehm was a rip-off artist, because he took 1 Prussian Thaler per day from us and for the trip to London we had to pay 9 Gulden and 15 Kreuzer. We left at 2 pm and arrived the next morning (Sunday 11 January) at 8 o'clock. That only took us 18 hours and no ship before has done that trip in such a short time.

As soon as we got to the North Sea the sea sickness started. Esselborn's Gertraud was the first, then Seyben Katchen (Kätchen Seyb), then Settchen Schwarz, but not so bad. All the others were spared. A tanner of Kreuznach, who travelled with us, was so seasick, that everyone was really fearful. When we arrived, Mr Tisch had sent somebody to pick us up and to bring us to our accommodation. We all got well looked after, only Meng, Findt and I had to stay "in eine Botic ersten Ranges" [untranslateable, might mean bad accommodation] where we had to stay only for one night. We moved to Mr Beisser where we lived in a happy bachelor community, with no warm meals and sleeping on the floor, but at least on our mattresses. Luckily we are all well and awake like rats and sing and jubilate day and night.

London is a city you cannot imagine. Only money! Money! Money! And sadly! God we lack of [we don't have it]. Poor like church-mice we jubilate and live in Dulci Jubilo. But tomorrow morning (15 January) that's going to have an end. We move onto our ship Sebastopol, which is an impressive three-mast-ship and if it moves as fast as the ship which brought us to London, it will only take 6 weeks and we are in New Zealand. But patience, it will not go so fast.

Tisch`s wife has a magnificent boy and is out of bed. It was just in time that he came, because only a day after our arrival she had her confinement. Esselborn's letter we received from Isaac Meyer....

And now live well and have friendly regards from your

K.F. Zinckgraf"[79]

There is no letter about the voyage itself, but the next surviving letter described the fortunes of the passengers a short time after arrival. It mentioned what employment the German passengers had in the first few months in Canterbury. Gertrude Esselborn was working in Papanui for a German. Katchen (Catherine) Seyb was with the German, Dr. Hast (likely Sir Johann Franz "Julius" von Haast). Karl Findt and Karl Meng were working out in the countryside and Dorothea Schmieh was about 30 miles away and he had not had contact with her since they arrived. Philipp Tisch had made some miscalculations with his business.[79] Karl Zinckgraf had been working as a music teacher in the homes of rich people as well as performing around Christchurch. He mentioned that, with a few dollars saved, a German could do very well in New Zealand, and he encouraged the readers of his letter to follow him.[79]

There was a man on board the *Sebastopol* from Germany named Arnold who does not appear on the passenger list but he signed an autograph for fellow passenger Elise Katharina Ellenberger (who obtained autographs from the German single men and women on the ship) and he signed it "Arnold v W." One explanation is that he was "Arnold von W" meaning Arnold from a village starting with the letter "W".

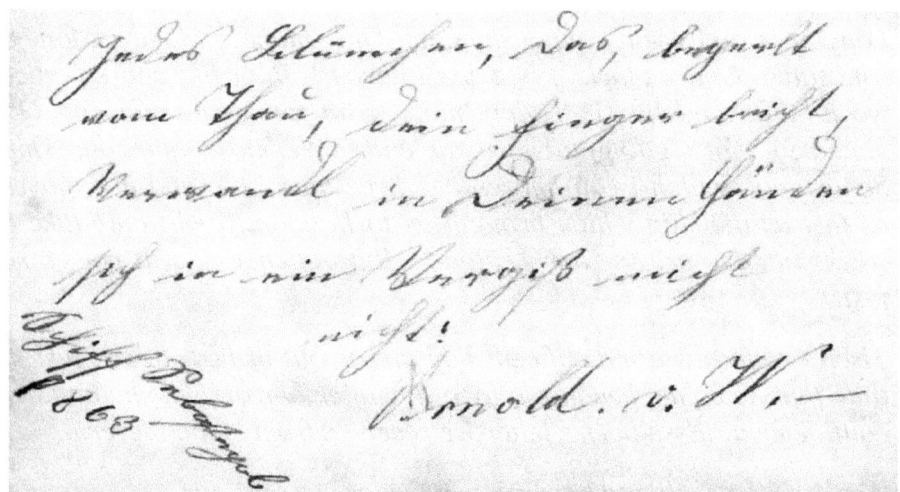

Notecard written by Arnold v. W on the "Schiff Sebastopol 1863." Elise Katharina Ellenberger collected autographs from some passengers. They are all similar, asking Jesus and God to take care of her and are possibly transcribed from a book they had on the ship.

A card from Katharina Seyb had a beautiful message which read:

Sebastopol im Mai 1863 K.S.

Wir hoffen jetzt an jenen Zauber bald zu sein
das in der Heimat uns
so lockend einst erschien!
O, mögen Dir nur lauter Rosen

in dem fernen Lande blühn
das beste Freundin was ich selbst mir wünschen kann
das sei, O Elise! Dir beschieden
dies wünscht von Herzen, Deine Freundin Katchen Seyb

We hope from now to find the magic soon
which in our homeland seemed to be so alluring
O, I wish you only roses
blooming in the far country
the best, friend, that I would wish for myself
that may, O Elise! happen to you
that wishes from you are heard, your friend Katchen Seyb

Ian Arnst, German Researcher in Christchurch, has a theory that the infant on the *Sebastopol* named Philippina Dappet (Deibert), was born to single mother Dina Mehnke. Philippina's real name was Lena Mehnke and she came to New Zealand with the Deibert family (incorrectly spelt Dappet in the passenger list). Ian thinks that mother Dina Mehnke, born about 1841, came out to New Zealand three years later as a member of the Ridder family on the *Blue Jacket* in October 1866. Mrs Ridder's maiden name was Mehnke, so Dina was related to them. Dina wouldn't have been allowed to board the *Blue Jacket* aged 25 with a baby in the single women's quarters. Therefore her baby was given into the care of Philipp and Marie Deibert. Once in New Zealand, Dina Mehnke married August Hofmeister, *Sebastopol* passenger, in 1868. The marriage did not last long as Dina Hofmeister died before October 1872. Lena grew up known to the Ridder family as cousin Lena Mehnke and married Martin Mehrtens. Parts of this story were passed down the Mehrtens family, but there is no documented proof as such.[80]

The German community helped each other once they arrived in New Zealand. Many went to the Christchurch Deutsche Kirche, which opened in 1872 on the corner of Montreal and Worcester Street where the Christchurch Art Gallery is now situated. Others spread throughout Canterbury and the rest of New Zealand. They were known as hard workers and were much respected for this trait in the 19th century.

The Suicide of Dr Galbraith

In the *Lyttelton Times* of Wednesday 3 June 1863 there is an article regarding a tragedy on Thursday 28 May 1863 onboard the *Sebastopol* that was still sitting in Lyttelton Harbour after the journey from England.[81]

"On Thursday afternoon, about two o'clock, intelligence reached the shore from the ship *Sebastopol* that the medical officer had taken poison, and a boat had come for assistance. Drs. Donald and Rouse were soon on the jetty, and on reaching the ship, found the unfortunate man dead. It was decided to hold an inquest before Wm. Donald, Esq., on board, on Friday morning, when the following gentlemen were sworn on the jury:—Mr. Renshaw (foreman), Messrs. Preece, Leslie, Brooke, Fyfe, Chapman, Mansfield, Genet, Stout, Gibbons, Walker, and Billins.

"After viewing the body, the first witness called was Mr. A. B. Gillis, who said: I know deceased, he is my second cousin. I first met him in Lyttelton on Monday last; it was in the afternoon; at the time I noticed that he was not at all well. I found that he had been drinking. He expressed a wish that I should not leave him. I took him to my lodgings; next morning he appeared to be much worse. He appeared delirious. I took him to Dr. Donald. He fancied that a black face was always looking at him through the window. He had various delusions. Dr. Donald requested me to look after him, and I promised I would do so. On Thursday morning we left to come off to the ship; when near the Canterbury Hotel he would have a glass of porter. He appeared to get worse after we got on board, I went on board with the intention to pack up his things for him, and I noticed amongst other bottles, one containing prussic acid, about one ounce, lying at the foot of the bed, which I placed in his private medicine chest. I had previously asked him what it was, and he told me. I think he must have got the bottle containing the prussic acid during the time that I was on board the schooner Herald, lying alongside. I was on board to get some lunch. I was absent about a quarter-of-an-hour. On my return, I found Dr. Galbraith at dinner. I went forward to his cabin, and in about an hour was startled by hearing a scream in the saloon. On proceeding there I found deceased in convulsions, and was informed that he had taken poison, and at once administered a copious dose of mustard and water. This did not produce vomiting, and he was dead in the course of a quarter-of-an-hour.

"Mrs. Jameson was the next witness called, and said: I am a passenger by the *Sebastopol*. I remember Dr. Galbraith coming on board yesterday morning with a gentleman. He took his dinner with us in the saloon. After dinner we had some conversation together about his son. He said he was afraid he would never see him again. I recommended him to be a teetotaler. He appeared to be very anxious about some letter he had written to his son we had often held similar conversations, and I had before recommended him not to drink. He had promised me that he would sign the pledge. In a short time he got a cup with some water in it, and took a bottle from out of his breast, and poured something into the cup and drank it. I noticed him do a similar thing before, and I thought it was quinine that he had in the bottle, for he had told me that he was in the habit of taking it to strengthen him. The Doctor then handed me his watch, and requested me to give it to his son. I said, "Doctor, what have you taken?" He did not speak, but nodded his head, and handed me the bottle. I ran with it to Mr. Greaves. Some mustard and water was given to make him vomit, but it did not do so, he died in a quarter-of-an-hour.

"By the Coroner: I had noticed that he was in rather low spirits at times during the voyage. I had reason to think that he used to drink. I did not see much of him except at the dinner table. I should think he had drink in his cabin at times. I think he must have known what he had taken.

"The Coroner said he should like to call Dr. Rouse to give his evidence as to the probable state of the mind of the deceased, as he had had opportunities of forming some opinion, having had to prescribe for him on one or two occasions since he came on shore.

"Dr. Rouse was then duly sworn, he said: I have seen Dr. Galbraith several times. On the first occasion he appeared to be suffering from great depression of spirits, and appeared to have been drinking. The second time he came he called very late, and looked very much worse. He was not actually in a state of delirium, but fast bordering on it. He had all the symptoms of a man suffering from excessive drinking. I saw him last Wednesday with his cousin at his lodgings. The medicine I had given to him had done him good. I last saw him on Thursday afternoon on board, in consequence of a message I received. I found deceased lying on his back on one of the benches. His body was quite warm, but he was dead. I should think he had taken half an ounce of prussic acid, judging from the quantity left in the bottle, and that indicated by the mate, who had seen it a day or two previously. That would be sufficient to kill eight or nine people. I found mustard and water had been administered to him, but without effect. I am quite of opinion that at the time he was in a state of mind not to be considered responsible for his actions. Dr. Donald accompanied me on board, and acquiesced with me in that opinion.

"Mrs. Jameson was recalled at the request of the jury to identify the bottle produced.

"The Coroner drew the attention of the jury to the circumstances of the case as adduced by the three witnesses, and thought that it was not necessary to call any further evidence.

"The jury acquiesced in the suggestion, and returned the following verdict—"That the deceased died from prussic acid administered by his own hand, but at a time when he was not master of his own actions.""

Charles John Galbraith was born in Hull, Yorkshire in 1823,[82] the eldest son of John Murray Galbraith M.D. and Charlotte Britannia Wimberley who married 10 April 1822 at Doncaster, York, England.[83] Charles is buried in Lyttelton in an unmarked grave in the Lyttelton Holy Trinity Anglican Cemetery.[44] His second cousin was mentioned in the inquest and probate as being Alexander Bayne Gillis. Gillis hadn't seen Charles for ten years until he landed at Lyttelton. Gillis eventually moved to Australia.

It seems that most alcohol-related deaths of the 1850s and 1860s in New Zealand were in the medical profession. The pressure of the job probably got to a lot of them. Doctors would often come out as a last ditch chance to regain sobriety and get their lives back.[84] In the case of Charles John Galbraith this last ditch chance didn't work.

Charles John Galbraith was highly educated and it appears he came from a good family, but none of this could help his alcoholism. In his inquest it stated that there was no family history of insanity but that his wife was insane.[73] In the 1851 census he was living with his mother Charlotte and his son Charles M. G. Galbraith, aged four. His wife was not with him. The pressures of having an ill wife, plus the pressures of his job may have led him to drink, but we can only guess at this. Charles had written a letter to his 18 year old son and had asked Jane Jameson to send it for him as well as his watch. We can guess that it would have been a kind of suicide note and farewell. One can only hope that the letter made sense as he was not in a good state of mind when he wrote it. It would have been upsetting for his son Charles who was living at Mt Hutt, Canterbury at the time of his father's probate in June 1863.[85] At age 18, Charles junior was a minor and the only next of kin, Alexander Bayne Gillis, was nominated as guardian of Charles senior's effects until Charles junior reached the age of 21 years. The estate in New Zealand and his personal effects were not above 50 pounds. Charles junior died aged 28 in England, an even more premature death than his father.[86]

Festivities in Lyttelton Harbour 7 July 1863

If Dr. Charles Galbraith had managed to stay sane and had not taken his own life he would have seen a magical sight in Lyttelton Harbour on 7 July 1863 while the *Sebastopol* still sat in port. The township decided to celebrate the marriage of The Prince of Wales to Princess Alexandra of Denmark. Edward and Alexandra married at St. George's Chapel, Windsor Castle, on 10 March 1863. Edward was 21; Alexandra was 18. Alexandra was renowned for her beauty and grace and was popular with the public.[87]

Princess Alexandra & The Prince of Wales on their wedding day

A full and detailed article was published in the Lyttelton Times on 15 July 1863 due to "great demand" from the public.

"Lyttelton was to show her loyalty on the 7th July, and right well it was done. The morning opened with genuine Queen's weather, at early dawn a signal gun reverberated across the harbour, by 8 o'clock clouds of bunting began to show on the ships and on shore; everybody appeared determined to give themselves up to a day of real enjoyment, each one trying in friendly competition to outvie his neighbour in display. Several handsome festal flags, adorned with flowers and evergreens, decorated the leading thoroughfares, and never before did the people of Lyttelton join in public festivities so general, so genial, and so enthusiastic. Animated by one common bond of strong instinctive loyalty, all classes joined spontaneously in the movement to evince their deep-seated attachment to our beloved Queen and the members of her family."

There was a large parade in the streets of Lyttelton, boat races, sports on the shore, and a public dinner held at the Church schoolroom. At night they had "The Illuminations" which was the lighting of shops and offices around Lyttelton. The Lyttelton Gaol was one of the main attractions with the initials of the Prince and Princess formed with Chinese lanterns as well as many other effects from the windows.

There were meant to be fireworks but the man responsible for them never arrived from Dunedin, so they never happened.

"The ships *Metropolis*, *Sebastopol*, and *Roman Emperor* lent their aid during the day to give éclat to the festivities and illuminations, besides discharging their big guns and firing innumerable rockets and blue lights."

The final item on the agenda was a ball which had about 100 attending at the Town Hall. The dancing went on until the morning."[88]

SHIP SEBASTOPOL.

ALL Claims against the above vessel must be rendered in duplicate on or before Tuesday 14th instant, otherwise they will not be recognized.

DALGETY, BUCKLEY, AND CO.,
Agents, Lyttelton.

Press, 3 July 1863

INQUEST.—An inquest was held at the Hospital, Christchurch, on the 27th inst., upon the body of Mrs. Elizabeth Baxter, who had lately arrived in the colony in the Sebastopol. The deceased had been confined a month since, on board ship, and shortly afterwards was so alarmed by one of her children having been scalded, that she had a fit of epilepsy, and continued in a very weak state. On arriving at Lyttelton she wished to go ashore, and an order having been procured she was sent off to the Hospital at Christchurch in a light cart. At Sumner she partook of refreshment, but shortly before she got to the Hospital she was found to be dead. Verdict—"Died by the Visitation of God."

Lyttelton Times, 30 May 1863

RESIDENT MAGISTRATE'S COURT.
(Before W. DONALD, Esq., R.M.)
Wednesday, July 1st.

Francis Pender, an apprentice of the ship Sebastopol, was charged with desertion, and ordered to be taken on board the ship.

Lyttelton Times, 8 October 1863

IF this should meet the eye of FRANCIS TISSOL a native of Switzerland, who is supposed to be in Canterbury, and who came to this province in the ship Sebastopol, he will meet with his brother at Mr P. Tisch, farmer, North Road, or if any person can give any information relating to said party to Mr. Dennise, hairdresser, Gloucester-street, they will oblige. 723

Press, 3 July 1863

SHIP SEBASTOPOL.

TAKEN from the said ship a CASE, addressed "Robt. Blackie, Christchurch."
Any information of the above will be thankfully received by Robert Blackie, Lyttelton. 4655

Lyttelton Times, 4 February 1864

A WEDDING SPOILED.—A rather stylish young person about 19 years of age, named Fanny Richards, was brought up on a warrant before the Resident Magistrate, on Thursday, upon a charge of obtaining goods under false pretences. It appears that the individual in question came up by the South mail from Timaru last week, and calling upon Mr. Adley, at the Oxford Hotel, gave him to understand that she was about to be married, and that her intended husband (whose name is Williams) was coming from Timaru immediately. Mr. Adley was asked to prepare the wedding breakfast, in compliance with which he gave extensive orders to Mr. Gee for a superb cake and other delicacies considered necessary on these occasions. Mr. Clarkson, draper, was also visited by the bride *in esse*, and a wedding dress valued at eleven guineas, and a bridal bonnet of the value of five guineas, were chosen. Mr. Clarkson not seeing the money forthcoming made some demur as to giving up the goods, but upon Miss Fanny saying it would be all right, and that her father and mother had arrived in Port by the Sebastopol, he allowed the goods to be taken away. The young lady having made these preparations, intimated her intention to Mr. Adley of proceeding to the Ashburton to meet her intended, and left for that purpose. She returned to the "Oxford" on Saturday last, and after dinner requested Mr. Adley to lend her a few shillings as she had exhausted her resources by paying Manning her fare from Timaru. The money was lent, and she started for Port to meet Mr. Williams, as no time could be lost, the wedding being fixed to take place on the Monday following. From certain discrepancies in her statement, Mr. Adley had his suspicions, and upon seeing Manning found that Miss Fanny had not paid him a farthing of her fare. Mr. Adley now determined to follow the fair one to Lyttelton, and ascertain what she was about. In detective phraseology "from information received," he went to a house occupied by parties named Roberts, where the young lady had been staying, and upon Mr. Adley inquiring there for her, he was taken to be the long expected bridegroom, Mr. Williams. In Miss Fanny's room were found a quantity of dresses, bonnets, wreaths of orange blossoms and other gay apparel, obtained from Mr. Hislop, draper; ivory-handled knives and forks, china vases, and other bric-à-brac, from various tradesmen; and lastly, some dozens of stout, pale ale, port, sherry, and a case of brandy, from the Mitre Hotel, to make merry withal. It is needless to say that these articles were obtained under the same representation as at Christchurch, and Miss Fanny must certainly possess fascinating powers of no mean order to have induced the tradesmen to trust her with their goods. Mr. Adley eventually met with the young lady and persuaded her to return to Christchurch, where she was apprehended on a warrant at the instance of Mr. Clarkson. The case was gone into before the Resident Magistrate, who ordered a remand till yesterday, to enable the Captain of the Sebastopol to be present to prove that the prisoner's statement, that her father and mother came out in the Sebastopol, was false. It was upon the strength of this statement that the prosecutor supplied the articles. The case was resumed on Friday morning; the Resident Magistrate considered there was sufficient evidence tendered to warrant him in committing the prisoner to take her trial at the Supreme Court.

Lyttelton Times, 13 June 1863

TESTIMONIAL TO CAPTAIN DUNCAN TAYLOR.—"We, the undersigned passengers on board the Sebastopol from London to Canterbury, N.Z., are desirous, before separating, to express to Captain Duncan Taylor our appreciation of his able and courteous conduct during the passage, and of our deep sense of his high talent and efficiency as a commander. His position was a difficult and arduous one, principally on account of the obstacles which arose through the very illiberal arrangements of the agents, Willis, Gann & Co., London, or the owners, but nothing prevented his utmost endeavors to promote the comfort and happiness of all on board. We shall never forget his watchfulness over the safety of ourselves and the ship while suffering from heavy and repeated gales in the Channel, his constant attention being given at the cost of rest during many successive nights and days, and we feel grateful that his health has been continued to him throughout the voyage. We are particularly anxious, also, to testify to Captain Duncan Taylor's great anxiety for the health of all—allaying the fears of the timid, speaking consoling words to the sick, and personally superintending the administration of all necessaries for the emigrants. Our sympathy was with him while, by a continuance of opposing winds, the vessel was hindered from making as quick a passage as we might otherwise have had. In addition to this expression of opinion, we beg to present to Captain Duncan Taylor a slight memento, in grateful recognition of his kindness, with best wishes for the future happiness and welfare of himself and family. May 16th, 1863." (Signed by 17 cabin, all the second cabin and steerage passengers, and crew.)

Lyttelton Times, 3 June 1863

SHIP SEBASTOPOL.

THE Commissioners are satisfied with all the arrangements of the ship. The immigrants are in good health, the ship in cleanly condition, the stores of good quality.

The immigrants express themselves well satisfied with the treatment they have received from the captain, surgeon, and officers of the ship.

                WM. DONALD,
                JOHN T. ROUSE,
                H. S. McKELLAR,
2343   F. E. WRIGHT.

Lyttelton Times, 23 May 1863

Passengers on the 1863 Voyage

Passengers on the 1863 Voyage

Anderson

William Anderson was born in 1843 at Dairy, Ayrshire, Scotland. He worked for his father on his Larnarkshire farm until he turned 20 when he decided to emigrate. He married Jane Baxter in 1862 and in 1863 they boarded the *Sebastopol* for New Zealand. His first job in New Zealand was working on the roads for the Provincial Government and then he delivered telegraph poles along the line from Riccarton to the Rangitata River. This was a dangerous job and he struck many floods and storms on the route. William bought land in the Cust area in 1864. He gradually added to the land until he had 1000 acres. He was very involved in community affairs, even after ill health that paralysed him down one side. William and Jane had six sons and four daughters. Four of his sons had their own farms at Rakaia, Mason's Flat, and North Loburn.[89]

Mr. W. Anderson

Billens

William Edgar Billens was listed as a gold chaser on the *Sebastopol* passenger list. He was born on 3 January 1824 in Westminster, London to Robert Billens and Esther Maria Woollams.[90] He appears in the Timaru Herald on 3 September 1873 as a carpenter living at Burkes Pass.[91] He died in New Zealand in 1906, aged 82.[92]

Deibert

Philipp Deibert of Osthofen, Germany and his wife Marie (née Tisch) were named on the passenger list as Dappet. The story passed down generations of the Mehrtens family is that the child with them on the *Sebastopol* named, Philippina Dappet, was actually Lena Mehnke the child of single mother Dinah Mehnke who came out to New Zealand in approximately 1866. Lena eventually married Martin Mehrtens.[80] Philipp and Marie settled in the North of Christchurch, in the Papanui/Styx area.[93] Marie died in 1874 aged 43 when the couple were living on the North Road, and was buried 23 October 1874 at St Paul's Papanui. Philipp remarried on 1 Feb 1875 to Mary Chernitska. They had at least one child but Mary died in 1877 aged 34. Philipp remarried for a third time to Ellen Theresa Reilly who was Catholic on 28 July 1877 where Philipp was listed as a farmer. They had at least two boys. Ellen died in 1901 aged 73 and Philipp died in 1914 aged 83. The name is often misspelt as Diebert, Dibert and other variants.[44]

Dinneen

Jeremiah Dinneen (sometimes spelt Dineen) was a bootmaker in Madras Street, Christchurch.[92] He married Mary Dinihan in 1866 and they had many children. It appears he moved to the Ashburton area in later life. He died in 1917 aged 80 years.[92]

Ellenberger

Jacob Nathanial Ellenberger was born in Friedelsheim, Palatinate, Germany on 9 May 1838; the son of a Mennonite Preacher. He travelled to New Zealand with his sister Elise Katharina Ellenberger, who was incorrectly named as Marie Ellenberger on the passenger list. Jacob married Marie Griebel on 15 January 1874. She arrived in 1870 on the *Zealandia*. Jacob and Marie lived at the Native Reserve, Tuahiwi, where Jacob was a farmer, and later on at Sneyd Street, Kaiapoi. Jacob died on 15 October 1910 and Marie on 27 November 1922. They had five sons and four daughters but the Ellenberger name did not continue in New Zealand beyond Jacob and Marie's children.[94]

Jacob and Marie Ellenberger with son Adolf c. 1875

Falloon

William James Falloon was born in Ballyleny townland, County Armagh, Ireland. He married Matilda Reid on 31 January 1865 at

Kaiapoi. William's occupation was labourer at the time. They had at least six children; four of them being Robert, Isabella, William Francis and Walter.[92] William senior died in 1897 and was buried in Christchurch. His wife Matilda died in 1914 and was buried in Waimate Cemetery.[95]

Findt

Karl Findt was born around 1842 and emigrated from the village of Kindenheim, Germany. Known as Charles, he was a farmer in the Westport area in the 1885 electoral rolls. He married Chatarina Maria Fredericke Bäumler in 1880. Charles died in 1908 and was buried at Orowaiti Middle Cemetery. Charles' wife, who was known as Mary, died in Christchurch in 1923.

Gardner/McKinley

George Glegg Gardner was born in Deal, Kent, England in 1845 and went to sea at an early age, working his way up to the position of third mate. He was in this position when he arrived as a crew member at Lyttelton on the *Sebastopol* in 1863. On arrival he was virtually engaged to a passenger from the ship, Margaret McKinley; a 19 year old dairymaid born in Newmains, Lanarkshire, Scotland. She had emigrated after a quarrel with her father's third wife. George was going to abandon ship but Margaret convinced him to return to England on the *Sebastopol*. He arrived back

Mrs. M. Gardner

in Lyttelton in March 1864. Margaret went to work for H. C. H Knowles at Glentui station (who was a cabin passenger on the *Sebastopol*), spending about a year there. Then she worked for Mrs Higgins, wife of the manager of Murphy's Run, Cust. George's first job in New Zealand was at the Customhouse at Lyttelton where he stayed for three years. He married Margaret in March 1866.

They bought land at Cust and lost the timber for their house in the 1868 flood, it being washed out to sea from Kaiapoi. They had about a few hundred acres of farm land and also a flour mill which they built in 1882. George died on the 5 February 1885, leaving six sons and four daughters.[96] He had a terrible accident while loading a rifle. Margaret then became a true feminist of her time. She managed both the farm and mill as well as raising her family. The mill became known as "Mrs Gardner's Mill." Her son Ralph took over the running eventually.[71] Margaret died on 19 June 1929 in Christchurch.

Innes

Frank Innes opened "The Rising Sun" hotel in St Albans in 1865 on what used to be the garden of Dr Augustus Florance. The hotel was infamously known as the "Rising Hell" and became the "Caledonian" in 1878, closing in 2007. It was going to be dug by archaeologists in 2009 but looters picked over the site. It is now covered in town houses.[97]

Innes Road in Christchurch is not named after Frank however, but a David Innes, a sheep farmer who at one stage owned a homestead on Papanui Road with 25 acres of land.[98]

Jameson

The Jameson family had seven members on board the *Sebastopol*. The following biographies are for three family members.

James Purvis Jameson was born in London in 1824. He married Jane Dyer Waugh in 1847. After arriving in New Zealand he was one of the first members of the Industrial Association of Canterbury and became the second president of the association. He was an original promoter of the Kaiapoi Woollen Company. He was a director of the Mutual Benefit Building Society for several years. He was also chairman of the Christchurch Public Cemetery Board. He was Mayor of the City of Christchurch in 1871 and a councillor for quite a few years. He was also in business as a merchant in Christchurch.

Mr W. Jameson

He bought a farm at Leeston soon after arriving, sold it and bought another farm at Coalgate where he resided during the latter part of his life. He died on 6 September 1896 and left a family of four sons and one daughter. [99]

William Jameson, the son of James Purvis Jameson, was born in 1849 in Manchester. He was educated at the local grammar school and then Dr Cranswick's school at Cheetham Hill. After arriving in New Zealand he became a clerk for the Provincial Secretary's office, was transferred to the public works office, then treasury, becoming sub-treasurer. When the provinces were abolished he was Provincial Treasurer of Canterbury. When the county system came in he was appointed clerk to the Selwyn County. He was a Fellow of the Institute of Incorporated Accountants of New Zealand. He was auditor of the New Zealand Farmer's Cooperative Association and some large private firms. He married the daughter of a Mr. James in 1877.[100]

James Samuel Jameson, the son of James Purvis Jameson was also born in Manchester, England. He was also educated at Rev. Dr Cranswick's school and the Manchester Grammar School before coming to New Zealand. He took up mercantile life and had responsible positions with Messrs. Gould and Miles, and Mr. George Gould, general merchants and station agents, Christchurch. In 1877 James started up his own business in Christchurch, and accepted the agency for the United Insurance Company, Limited, for Canterbury which he held for 14 years. When the company reorganised its business in 1891 he obtained the responsible position of Resident Secretary for New Zealand. This meant he had to move to Wellington.

Kippenberger

Georg Peter Kippenberger (known as Peter) was born in Kindenheim, Germany. He married Barbara Mann on 10 June 1845, in Kindenheim. Barbara was born about 1823 in Kriegsheim, Germany. Peter began life in New Zealand as a farm labourer. He died 24 February 1881 at Washdyke Flat near Timaru in an accident in which he was dragged by a horse. Barbara died ten years later in Christchurch, 6 September 1891 of heart failure at the age of 68.

They had eleven children, two of whom died as infants. The three youngest were born in New Zealand. The Kippenberger name was made famous by Sir Howard Kippenberger, a renowned soldier and military historian of World War II, who reached the rank of Major-General. He lived in Rangiora where Kippenberger Ave was named after him. There are around 800 descendants for this family in New Zealand.[101]

Kissel

Heinrich Kissel was born on 10 October 1828 in Grosskarlbach, Germany. He travelled with his two brothers to America supposedly to escape the German Military Regime. He returned to Germany prior to 1859 when he married Philippina Stocke.

Heinrich and family were travelling on his American passport when they came to New Zealand; it is stamped 3 January 1863, London. Twins Barbara and Henry were born 11 Sept 1860 and Elizabeth was born 9 Nov 1862 prior to the family's departure from Germany. Barbara does not appear on the ship's list while her twin sibling Henry and sister Elizabeth are listed.

Heinrich Kissel

Heinrich's brother, Wilhelm, had already reached New Zealand, sailing for Canterbury on *Midlothian* arriving at Lyttelton on 8 October 1851. Wilhelm was a saddler and is reputed to have opened the first saddlery in Christchurch.

Heinrich and Philippina had two more daughters in New Zealand, Anna and Katherine (Kate). The family lived at Hazeldean Road, Sydenham, Christchurch. Philippina died in 1884 and Heinrich mid 1900. They are buried in Addington Cemetery, Christchurch.

Philippina Kissel née Stocke

Knowles

Haderezer Charles Henderson Knowles first came to New Zealand around October 1853. He took up the Glentui Run (Run 145) in December 1854 and ran it until 1875. It was a run of five thousand acres (a small run) with about 1400 sheep. The Glentui Run lay on the foothills between Ashley Gorge and the Tui Creek and ran back to the Harewood Forest Reserve.[102] H.C.H Knowles and his new wife, Isabella Falcon Knowles (née Leech), who he married in 1862 in Whitehaven, Cumbria, England, were cabin passengers on the *Sebastopol*. They employed fellow passenger Margaret McKinley on their run for about a year after they arrived back on the *Sebastopol*. Isabella died in 1871 in New Zealand and Mr Knowles married again in 1872 to Elizabeth Whittem. H.C.H Knowles died in 1879 aged a young 46 years old.

Latto

James Latto, son of William Latto and Barbara Ross, was born around 24 February 1828 in Kinglassie, Fife, Scotland. He married Mary Brown on 31 Dec 1847 in Markinch, Fife, Scotland. They had five children, Catherine, William, George, James and David, all born in Markinch, Scotland. Catherine died before they travelled to New Zealand and James junior died not long after they arrived in their new land. James senior and Mary had land at West Eyreton, North Canterbury. Mary Latto died on 5 Nov 1888 and James Latto senior died on 20 May 1907. They are buried in Cust – West Eyreton Public Cemetery. [103]

Loney

Ann Loney was from County Armagh, Ireland, and travelled on the *Sebastopol* at age 17. She married Alfred Ford a year after she arrived and they had four children, Evelyn, Ada, Harry and Ernest. Ann and Alfred were involved in dairy farming at Rapaki and used to carry their produce over the hill to Christchurch as there was no Lyttelton Tunnel back then. They eventually settled in Papanui, Christchurch. Ann lived until she was 90 years old.

Meng/Ellenberger

Karl Philipp Meng (27 June 1834 to 1885) came from a farming family of Hohen-Sülzen, Germany. He married fellow *Sebastopol* passenger Elise Katharina Ellenberger of Friedelsheim, Germany, in Christchurch in 1866 and had seven daughters, of which only three survived to maturity. Hellene drowned in a waterhole in Tuahiwi aged two. Lina and Amelia were twins who died at three and four months respectively of malnutrition. Elise Mary died of pneumonia aged 12. Karl farmed at the Maori Reserve at Tuahiwi and then bought a farm at Ohoka around 1871. Elise died in 1879 after having a stillborn child. Karl married widow Sarah Winfield Potts (née Brown). Karl and Elise Meng are buried in the Flaxton Cemetery with three of their children.[104]

Karl Philipp & Elise Katharina Meng (née Ellenberger) c. 1866

Pollock

William Pollock, born 1841 in Lesmahagow, Larnarkshire, Scotland, married Ann Rodger (born 1839 in Lesmahagow) on 30 December 1862 in Lesmahagow. They boarded the *Sebastopol* a short time after bound for New Zealand. William and Ann spent a short time in Dunedin and the Taieri before settling in Shag Valley around 1867. In 1884 he leased some land in the Shingley Creek district and eventually bought a freehold property of 200 acres. William bred Ayrshire cattle. William and Ann had six sons and one daughter.[105]

Ann died 9 June 1915 and William died 8 September 1924 both in Waikaka, Southland. They are buried at Gore, Southland.

Ruddock

Edward Ruddock was born in Armagh, Ireland in 1839. After arriving on the *Sebastopol* he looked around Canterbury and then took up a manager position at Beechcroft Estate, Southbridge, working for Mr. Jollie, Provincial Secretary. Edward stayed in the position until 1867 and then purchased his own farm of 366 acres, which was partly in tussock and in a wild state. He drained and fenced the property and did other improvements. It was called *Fieldmont*. Later he leased two other areas of 477 and 391 acres, and then had large sheep farming and mixed farming operations. He bred Shorthorn cattle and received first prizes at various shows. He was a member of the Ellesmere Road Board but gave up due to ill health. He was a member of the Ellesmere Agricultural and Pastoral Association, and won prizes for draught horses. Edward was also a member and shareholder of the New Zealand Farmers' Co-operative Association. Edward Ruddock married in Ireland. He and his wife had a family of nine children; four sons and four daughters were alive around 1903.[106]

Mr E. Ruddock

Seyb

Katharina Seyb, known as Catherine, was from Kindenheim, Germany, born in about 1839. After travelling to New Zealand on the *Sebastopol*, she married Henry Aker (a butcher originally from Wurttenburg, Germany), on 21 December 1864 at Holy Trinity, Avonside, Christchurch. They had many children up until 1879 including twin boys in 1869 when Henry was named as a milkman at the time.[107] The family moved to Washdyke, Timaru. Catherine died in 1879 and Henry in 1908.[108]

Thorne

William Henry Thorne was born in Newnham, Gloucestershire, England in 1845 and sailed to New Zealand on the *Sebastopol* aged 17. He travelled with his future sister-in-law Elizabeth Grace Watts. He leased land from 1869 for years adjoining the Heathcote River. In 1876 he was listed as a coal merchant and was declared bankrupt in 1879, when he was listed as a farmer. He died in 1907 after drowning in the Heathcote River at Woolston. The police found him after dragging the river. There were five children living at the time of his death.[109]

Tisch

Philipp Tisch and his wife Christina (née Vogt) were from Kindenheim, Germany. They left the Downs, United Kingdom on 22 June 1851 and sailed to New Zealand with the Kissel family on the *Midlothian,* arriving 8 October 1851 with 4 children. They settled in Lyttelton. Their two little girls died in 1851. Susanna on 23 October 1851 and no date other than 1851 for Magdalena so it is suspected she died at sea. Shortly after their arrival in New Zealand, he farmed on 50 acres of Church property between the Styx & Kapitone Creek for 5 years. Later, they purchased land still known as "Tisch's Corner," on the North Road near Belfast and kept on buying land until he had about 700 acres. Seeing the great demand for sawn timber in a new colony, he also started a sawmill in Christchurch with Mr Neece. The demand for sawn timber increased and to keep up the supply Philipp purchased a large tract of forest land at Alford Forest. He erected a sawmill and the Alford Forest Hotel, (which still remains) and also the Spreadeagle Hotel where he flew the Imperial German flag, which had the insignia of the Spreadeagle. In 1862 when he had news of his father's death, he returned to Bavaria and recruited 15 family and friends. He also recruited females for the German men in New Zealand, for which he received payment from the Provincial Council. He returned with his widowed mother Christina on the *Sebastopol*. His youngest son Albert, was born in January 1863, just before the voyage set sail, and died in March 1864. Philipp was also involved in setting up the German Church in Worcester Street, Christchurch and his name was engraved on the foundation stone on November 1872 with 4 other names. He was elected President of the German Church in 1873. He was chairman of the Belfast School community 1869-1874 and donated the land for the new school, which opened in 1878. He was chairman of the Avon Road Board, a vestryman of St Paul's, Papanui and a director of the Brewing, Malting & Distilling Co. In 1878 his wife Christina died. He remarried in 1884 to Ann Williams Kerr, a widow, until his death in 1892.[110]

Watts

Elizabeth Grace Watts was born about 1843 in England. She emigrated aged 20 on the *Sebastopol* with William Henry Thorne, marrying his brother Frederick Thorne later in 1863. Elizabeth and Frederick lived in Rangiora and owned land on Northbrook Road and East Belt in 1880. Her husband died in 1880 and the land was passed to her. Her house was destroyed by fire in 1908 and even her pig sty burnt down with pigs inside. The family had to escape at night in their night attire. Elizabeth died aged 72 in Rangiora.[111]

Whyte

William Whyte was born in Perthshire, Scotland in 1840. He travelled to New Zealand aged 23 with his parents, William and Elizabeth Whyte (née Bryce), and siblings. William worked in different parts of the country, including on a farm in Fendalton owned by William Boag. In 1868 he bought fifty acres of land and increased this to 180 acres. He kept sheep and cattle. He married Mary Ann Pigram (Peagram) of Surrey, England in 1868 and they had a surviving family of six sons and two daughters.[112]

Peter Whyte, brother to William Whyte, was born in Perthshire, Scotland in 1842 and came to NZ with his parents in 1863 on the *Sebastopol*. Peter settled in Halkett and his farm of 200 acres was called *Fairview*. He also owned another farm near Aylesbury of 225 acres and worked both of them at the same time. He grew oats and wheat as well as turnips and rape for fattening sheep. He married Mary Jane Butler in 1880, daughter of John Butler of Dunsandel, and they had four daughters and four sons.

Widdop

Jabez and Margaret Widdop, née Thompson, had five children baptized in Keighley, York on 17 Feb 1858, Henry, Margaret, Florinda, Lilla and Rosina. When they came out to New Zealand on the *Sebastopol* they had four children with them including a new child William aged three, Margaret and Rosina probably having died earlier. There seems to be no record of the family in New Zealand, but their son Henry, born 14 Sep 1850, died in Lawrence, Massachusetts, USA on 7 Oct 1913.[113]

Zinckgraf

Charles Albert Zinckgraf was born "Carl Albert" on 23 March 1832 in Biedesheim, Germany but lived in Kindenheim, Germany at the time of his emigration. He married Magdalena Clara Kissel on 4 May 1864 in Christchurch, New Zealand, and had 5 children. Charles was described as a Schoolmaster on the passenger list and apparently was in charge of a choir in Kindenheim. He was a pianist in Christchurch in the 1860s, and played at various concerts and entertainments, and helped at the Theatre Royal when they needed music. He also had a dance band. In March 1868 he supplied the music for a ball given by Capt Rose on the *Mermaid*. He was the pianist when the Philharmonic Soc. performed Handel's Samson in October 1869. Charles became ill in 1872 and died in his home at Tuam Street in 1873. His wife remarried William Clarke Fleming. When Charles died, he left 5 children and his wife totally unprovided for. At the time of his death his youngest child was age one and the oldest Charles Albert (named after his father) age 13.[114]

Passengers on the 1863 Voyage

Passenger Lists

Passenger Lists

The following lists have been transcribed directly from the passenger lists of steerage passengers, with cabin passengers taken from newspaper articles. Corrections were made after research was done on the passengers. The original transcriptions are in square brackets beside the correct spelling. There may still be errors in the list which render some names too different to the real people who landed in New Zealand. The 1863 list in particular was quite incorrect and has many missing names.

Passengers 1861					
Crew				
Surname	*Given Name*	*Age*	*Location*	*Occupation/ Notes*
Fraser	James Archibald			Commander
Chief Cabin				
Surname	*Given Name*	*Age*	*Location*	*Occupation/ Notes*
Batt	Mr and Mrs and child			
Bennett	Mrs and Miss			
Marshall	Miss			
Poigndestre	Mr and Mrs			
Thomson	Mrs and two children			
Willes [Willis]	Mr William			
Tanner	Mr			
Batt	Mr			
Boyd	Mr			
Mytton	Mr			
Second Cabin				
Surname	*Given Name*	*Age*	*Location*	*Occupation/ Notes*
Hagley	Mr			

Wrentmore	Mr			
Shrewry	Mr Thomas			
Smith	Mr G.			
Batten	Mr			
Sandrey [Saudry]	Mr George			
Smith	Mr. J			

Enclosed Steerage

Surname	Given Name	Age	Location	Occupation/ Notes
Muriso	Miss			
Vollans	Miss			
Jenkinson	Mr			
Raffen	Mr			
Crosbie	Mr			
King (2)	Mr			
Barnsley	Mr			
Vollans	Mr			

Government Immigrants

Married Couples

Surname	Given Name	Age	Location	Occupation/ Notes
Armstrong	Walter	24	Westmoreland	Blacksmith
	Dorothy	22		
Bird	Thomas	23	Westmoreland	Farm Labourer
	Mary	20		
Briscoe	James	31	Shropshire	Farm Labourer
	Caroline M. A.	33		
	Caroline M. A.	8		
	Eliza	6		
	Hannah	4		
	Lucy	1		
Clark	Donald	43	Invernesshire	Shepherd

		Isabella	34		
		Janet	8		
		James	6		
		John	4		
		Wilhelmina	9 mths		
Conner	Michael		King's County	Farm Labourer
	Wife and child			
Dempster	William	32	Antrim	Farm Labourer
	Mary	34		
	Mary E.	1		
Dethier	Theodore	42	Middlesex	Carpenter
	Jane	37		
	Theodore	3		
	Edward	1		
	Louisa	3mths		
Dickson	James	27	Lanarkshire	Ploughman
	Mary	20		
Dobson	Robert	32	Middlesex	Bootmaker
	Sarah Ann	35		
	Mary Ann	1		
Eaton	James	30	Yorkshire	Farm Labourer
	Hannah	32		
Eckhoff	Henry	46	Hanover	Farm Labourer
	Wilhelmina	36		
Elliott	Joseph	25	Lanarkshire	Ploughman
	Mary Jane	26		
Fabling [Fablin]	William	31	Kent	Cowkeeper
	Margaret	29		
	William	9		
	David	7		
	Henry	3		
	Margaret	3mths		
	Jane	7		*Sister*

Ferguson	George	26	Perthshire	Carpenter
	Marjory	20		
	Margaret	2		
	George	8 mth		
Greig	John	25	Rosshire	Shepherd
	Christina	26	Invernesshire	
Heuze	Henry	38	Hanover	Farm Labourer
	Johanne	28		
Haynes	John	25	Leicestershire	Farm Labourer
	Sarah Ann	25		
	Thomas	2		
	William	10 Mths		
Howell	Edmund	31	Staffordshire	Iron Moulder
	Sarah	31		
Hughes	James	27	Tyrone	Farm Labourer
	Sarah	21		
Hunter	Robert	38	Aberdeenshire	Sawyer
	Barbara	36		
	Elizabeth	9		
Johnson	Thomas	43	Nottingham-shire	Farm Labourer
	Mary	42		
	Ann	21	T/F to Single women	
	Elizabeth	20	T/F to Single women	
	Martha	18	T/F to single women	
	Samuel	17	T/F to single men	
	Sarah	14	T/F to single women	
	Fanny	11		
	Emma	5		
	Lucy	1		
	Joseph	1		
Ligget	Robert	24	Armagh	Farm Labourer

	Mary			
	Infant			
Lusk	David		Buteshire	Joiner
	Wife & 3 children			
Mason	John	26	Westmoreland	Farm Labourer
	Margaret	23		
	Jane	Infant		
Matthews	John	46	Oxfordshire	*Schoolmaster to Ship*
	Emma	29		
	Mary	9		
Noonan	Thomas	21	Lancashire	Carver
	Emma J.	18		
	Theresa	3 mth		
O'Shaughnessy	William	28	Kildare	Farm Labourer
	Mary	27		
Power	Michael	24	Waterford	Farm Labourer
	Mary	22		
	John	8 mth		
Power	John	24	Tipperary	Domestic Servant
	Alice	22		
Rainey	Robert	20	Antrim	Farm Labourer
	Mary	21		
Rockett	Thomas	28	Dorsetshire	Farm Labourer
	Elizabeth	29		
	Frederick	1		
	Emma	6 wks		
Round	Elijah	36	Staffordshire	Blacksmith
	Grace	35		
	Hannah	16	T/F to single women	
	Ebenezer	14	T/F to single men	
	Louisa	9		
Thomas	Charles	44	Gloucestershire	Butcher

	Elizabeth	45		
	Anne	20	T/F to single women	
	Robert	16	T/F to single men	
	Elizabeth	11		
	Mary	7		
Wills	Richard	36	Staffordshire	Farm Labourer
	Amelia	40		
	David	13	T/F to single men	
	Stephen	10		
	Peter	8		
	Amelia	3		

Single Men

Surname	*Given Name*	*Age*	*Location*	*Occupation/ Notes*
Adams	David	30	Down	Farm Labourer
Angus	Alexander	29	Clackmannan-shire	Labourer
Arnott	Robert	40	Armagh	Farm Labourer
Arnott	Thomas	20	Armagh	Farm Labourer
Brough	William	32	Perthshire	Farm Labourer
Collier	John	20	Carlow	Farm Labourer
Connor	Cornelius	29	Cork	Farm Labourer *Travelling with Hickey*
Connor or Comer	Edward John	20	Middlesex	Farm Labourer
Cassin	Michael	25	Queen's County	Farm Labourer
Davidson	Alexander	21	Aberdeenshire	Farm Labourer
Donovan	Cornelius	21	Cork	Labourer
Dunne	Martin	21	Galway	Ploughman
Falloon	Arthur	28	Armagh	Ploughman
Farquar	John	19	Armagh	Ploughman
Hazlehurst	John	29	Nottinghamshire	Farm Labourer
Hayward	William	30	Brecknockshire	Farm Labourer
Hayes	William	27	Down	Farm Labourer

Hayes	John	18	Down	Farm Labourer
Hickey	Cornelius	28	Cork	Farm Labourer *Travelling with C. Connor*
Johnson	Samuel	17	Nottinghamshire	Farm Labourer
Kerr	Edward	16	Midlothian	Shepherd
Kerr	Henry	14	Midlothian	Shepherd
Kerr	Henry	40	Midlothian	Blacksmith
Keenan	Michael	19	Fermanagh	Labourer
Lalor	Daniel	28	Queen's County	Farm Labourer
Lalor	Michael	22	Queen's County	Farm Labourer
Lord	William	20	Yorkshire	Labourer
Lowry	Robert	19	Down	Schoolmaster
May	George	30	Somersetshire	Labourer
McFarlane	Thomas	19	Down	Farm Labourer
McLachlan	John	22	Buteshire	Bricklayer
Milne	Alexander	19	Forfarshire	Carpenter
Moorhead	Michael	25	Down	Farm Labourer
Noonan	George	17	Lancashire	Labourer
Pope	John	36	Lanarkshire	Blacksmith
Rennie	Andrew	21	Perthshire	Farm Labourer
Rennie	John	19	Perthshire	Carpenter
Round	Ebenezer	14	Staffordshire	Farm Labourer
Ruddock	Edward	21	Armagh	Farm Labourer
Russell	Archibald	22	Argyleshire	Shepherd
Saunders	Benjamin	22	Gloucestershire	Gardener
Steele	Samuel	22	Londonderry	Ploughman
Tennant	Thomas	23	Carlow	Farm Labourer
Tennant	John	21	Carlow	Farm Labourer
Thomas	Robert	16	Gloucestershire	Farm Labourer
Wills	David	13	Staffordshire	Labourer
Wilson	John	23	Armagh	Farm Labourer
Wilson	James	20	Armagh	Farm Labourer
Wilson	Meredith	22	Armagh	Farm Labourer
Zuppicich	Antonio	20	Austria	*Not on original passenger list*

Single Women				
Surname	*Given Name*	*Age*	*Location*	*Occupation/ Notes*
Almond	Sarah	17	Middlesex	Dom. Servant
Brown	Caroline C.	18	Oxfordshire	Dom. Servant
Cook	Maria	30	Somersetshire	Cook
Crake	Eliza	19	Oxfordshire	Dom. Servant *Travelled with Matthews fam.*
Campbell	Elizabeth	15	Oxfordshire	Dom. Servant
Daley	Julia	18	Glamorganshire	Dom. Servant
Falloon	Elizabeth	26	Armagh	Dom. Servant
Geoike	Adeilheirh	28	Hanover	Cook
Hopkins	Sarah Jane	17	Gloucestershire	Domestic Servant
Johnson	Ann	21	Nottinghamshire	Dom. Servant
Johnson	Elizabeth	20	Nottinghamshire	Dom. Servant
Johnson	Martha	18	Nottinghamshire	Dom. Servant
Johnson	Sarah	14	Nottinghamshire	Dom. Servant
Lewis	Martha	49	Staffordshire	Nurse *Matron on ship*
May	Mary Ann	27	Gloucestershire	Dom. Servant
May	Alice Blanche	3	Gloucestershire	*Daughter of Mary May*
McKeown	Elizabeth	19	Londonderry	Needlewoman
McKeown	Margaret	17	Londonderry	Dom. Servant
McKeown	Mary	15	Londonderry	Dom. Servant
McKeown	Rachel	12	Londonderry	Dom. Servant
Moorhead	Mary Ann	21	Down	Dom. Servant
Power	Barbara	45	Waterford	Housekeeper
Power	Catherine	14	Waterford	Dom. Servant
Read	Mary	21	Aberdeenshire	Dom. Servant
Rennie	Isabella	45	Perthshire	Farm Servant
Rennie	Ann	25	Perthshire	Dom. Servant
Riddell	Sarah	20	Armagh	Dom. Servant
Round	Hannah	16	Staffordshire	Dom. Servant

Ruddock	Margaret	23	Armagh	Dom. Servant
Thomas	Annie	20	Gloucestershire	Dom. Servant
Toppin	Margaret	23	Waterford	Dom. Servant
Ward	Elizabeth	22	Leicestershire	Dom. Servant
Wheeler	Anne	29	Oxfordshire	Dom. Servant
Wheeler	Fanny	27	Oxfordshire	Dom. Servant
Woodward	Esther A.	25	Middlesex	Dom. Servant
Unconfirmed Passengers				
Kindley	William B			*Two letters not claimed. Lyttelton Times 23 April 1862*[115]
Percival	T			*Letter not claimed. Lyttelton Times 23 April 1862*[115]

Passengers 1863

Crew

Surname	Given Name	Age	Location	Occupation/ Notes
Taylor	Captain Duncan			Commander
Galbraith	Dr Charles John			Ships Surgeon
Greeves	Mr W. R.			Chief Officer
Gardner	George Glegg			Third Mate
Pender	Francis			Apprentice

Chief Cabin

Surname	Given Name	Age	Location	Occupation/ Notes
Bailiff	Miss Fanny			
Bedford	Mr			
Blackie	Mr (Robert)			
	Mrs			
Doyle	Mr C.			
Knowles	Mr (Haderezer Charles Henderson)			
	Mrs Isabella			
Harvey	Mr H. O.			
Jameson	J. P. (James Purvis)			
	Mrs Jane			
	James			
	William			
	George			
	Frederick			
	Jane			
Procter	Edward			

Passenger Lists

Surname	Given Name			
Stanley	Mr R.J.			
Second Cabin				

Surname	Given Name	Age	Location	Occupation/ Notes
Ashwin [Ashmin]	Helen			
	Mary			
Ashwin	Martin			
	Emma			
	Craven			
	Helen			
	Mary			
	Martin			
	Lilly			
Tisch [Fisher]	Philip			
	Christina			
	David			*No Tisch child was named David*
	Eliza			
	Maria			
	Albert			*Born 12 January 1863*
Hooper	Mr			
	Mrs			
Pearce	John			
	Sarah			
	John			
	Elizabeth			
	William			
	Thomas			
Smithson	Elizabeth			
Walters	Sarah			
	Annie			
Walters	W.			

Surname	Given Name	Age	Location	Occupation/Notes
Wheeler	Miss Sarah E.			

Enclosed Steerage

Surname	Given Name	Age	Location	Occupation/Notes
Buxton	John			
	Elizabeth			
	Sarah			
	Fanny			
Collier	Jonathan			
Tucker	Sarah			
	Willie			

Government Immigrants

Married Couples

Surname	Given Name	Age	Location	Occupation/Notes
Anderson	William	19	Lanarkshire	Ploughman
	Jane	21		
Baxter	William	25	Antrim	Farm Labourer
	Ellen	24		
	William	4		
Baxter	John			
	Elizabeth			*Died on arrival*
	Children			*One scalded on board*
	Elizabeth Ann	Infant		*Born on board 25 April 1863*
Blakeley	William John	44	Down	Labourer
	Mary	43		
	Jane	20	T/F to single women	*Travelled with Burke*
Bryant	William	24	Gloucestershire	Farm Labourer
	Louisa	19		Wife
Byrne	Thomas	24	Wicklow	Labourer

	Ann	20		*Travelled with Patrick Byrne*
Burke	William	28	Down	Labourer
	Rebecca	26		*Travelled with Blakeley*
Campbell	James	24	Antrim	Farm Labourer
	Mary Ann	25		
	Mary Jane	4 mth		
Croft	James	30	Bedfordshire	Smith
	Mary	33		
Cusack	Patrick	31	Clare	Tailor
	Catherine	30		
	Thomas	11		
	Martin	6		
	Bridget	6 mth		
Deibert [Dappet]	Philip	27	Germany	Farm labourer
	Mary	27		
	Phillipina	Infant		*Unconfirmed but thought to be Lena Mehnke*
Gardener	Andrew	49	Fifeshire	Farm Labourer
	Euphemia	45		
	Elizabeth	22	T/F to single women	
	Hugh	20	T/F to single men	
	John	18	T/F to single men	
	Andrew	16	T/F to single men	
	Margaret	8		
Hamilton	George	39	Lanarkshire	Ploughman
	Mary	40		
	Janet	9		
	Mary	5		*Travelled with Pollock and Brown*

	George	4		
Hooper	Francis	23	Middlesex	Bootmaker
	Emma H	22		Wife
Johnson	Thomas	41	Gloucestershire	Farm Labourer
	Charlotte	46		Wife
	Sarah A.	21	T/F to single women	
	James	16	T/F to single men	
	Maria	11		
	Thomas	8		
Johnson	George	22	Gloucestershire	Farm Labourer
	Ann	20		Wife
Kissel	Heinrich	34	Germany	Carpenter
	Phillipina	29		Wife
	Henry	2		
	Barbara	2		*Confirmed by descendants*
	Elizabeth	7 wks		
Latto	James	34	Fifeshire	Ploughman
	Mary	36		Wife
	William	9		
	George	7		
	James	5		
	David	3		
Legg	James	23	Antrim	Farm Labourer
	Mary	23		
	Edward	7 mths		
Kippenberger [listed as **Lippenberger**]	Peter	40	Germany	Farm Labourer
	Barbara	30		
	Gertrude	17	T/F to Single women	
	Katherine	15	T/F to Single women	
	Charles	11		

	Magdalene	9		
	Philip	7		
	Elizabeth	4		
Maltman	Andrew	47	Perthshire	Ploughman
	Elizabeth	36		
	~~William~~	~~17~~	~~T/F to single men~~	
	Andrew	11		
	Betsy	9		
Pollock	William	22	Lanarkshire	Ploughman
	Ann	24		*Travelled with Hamilton*
Ruddock	Edward	22	Antrim	Farm Labourer
	Ann	23		*Travelled with Hutcheson and Hall*
Scott	William	41	Lanarkshire	Farm Labourer
	Marion	40		
	John	22	T/F to single men	
	George	19	T/F to single men	
	Thomas	18	T/F to single men	
	Agnes	13	T/F to single women	
	Mary	11		
	Frank	8		
	William	3		
Todd	James	26	Lanarkshire	Carpenter
	Elizabeth	26		Wife
	William	4		
	Alexander	2		
Widdop	Jabez	35	Yorkshire	Plasterer
	Margaret	35		
	Henry	14	T/F to single men	

		Florinda	10		
		Lilly	5		
		William	3		
Whyte		William	43	Perthshire	Farm Labourer
		Margaret	43		
		William	23		T/F to single men
		Peter	21		T/F to single men
		James	19		T/F to single men
		Robert	17		T/F to single men
		Janet	9		
		Adam	6		

Single Men

Surname	*Given Name*	*Age*	*Location*	*Occupation/ Notes*
Addie [Adie]	John T.	23	Aberdeenshire	Farm Labourer
Aldridge	Albert	19	Gloucestershire	Labourer
Armitage	William	17	Lancashire	Labourer
Banks	Donald	22	Caithness	Farm Labourer
Bear	James P.		Oxfordshire	Schoolmaster *Schoolmaster to ship*
Billens	William E.	38	Middlesex	Gold Chaser
Brown	David	22	Lanarkshire	Ploughman *Travelled with Pollock and Hamilton*
Byrne	Patrick	26	Wicklow	Labourer
Dinneen	Jeremiah	23	Cork	Farm Labourer
Ellenberger	Jacob	26	Germany	Baker
Falloon	William J	21	Armagh	Farm Labourer
Findt	Charles (Karl)	21	Germany	Farm Labourer
Gardner	Hugh	20	Fifeshire	Farm Labourer
Gardner	John	18	Fifeshire	Farm Labourer

Gardner	Andrew	16	Fifeshire	Farm Labourer
Hofmeister	Henry	24	Germany	Carpenter
Hofmeister	Charles	22	Germany	Bootmaker
Hausmann [Houseman]	William	22	Germany	Dyer
Hooper	Stephen	21	Dorsetshire	Labourer
Innes	Frank	28	Caithness	Ploughman
Johnson	James	15	Gloucestershire	Labourer
Johnston	George James	22	Yorkshire	Labourer
Lemmon	John	24	Banffshire	Labourer
Loney	Joseph	19	Armagh	Farm Labourer
Maher	James	22	Queen's County	Labourer
~~**Maltman**~~	~~William~~	~~17~~	~~Perth~~	~~Ploughman~~
McDonald	James	32	Invernesshire	Shepherd
McInnes	Donald	25	Ayrshire	Ploughman
McInnes	John	27	Ayrshire	Ploughman
McKay	Alexander	?	?	?
Meng [Menges]	Karl Philipp [Jacob]	27	Germany	Farm Labourer
Milne	Alexander	33	Kincardineshire	Ploughman
Murray	James	30	Millwright	Lanarkshire
Murray	Thomas	27	Banffshire	Labourer
Murray	Roderick	?	?	?
Neiss	Frederick	25	Germany	Farm Labourer
Newman	William Henry	20	Middlesex	Cutler
Nicolson	Angus	26	Invernesshire	Farm Labourer
Robinson	Thomas	26	Yorkshire	Farm Labourer
Ruddock	William	17	Armagh	Farm Labourer
Schwartz	Jacob	44	Germany	Butcher
Scott	John	22	Lanarkshire	Tailor
Scott	George	19	Lanarkshire	Farm Labourer
Scott	Thomas	18	Lanarkshire	Farm Labourer
Stephenson	Christopher	25	Durham	Bricklayer

Thorne [Thorn]	William Henry	17	Gloucestershire	Tanner
Treleaven	James	25	Devonshire	Farm Labourer
Widdop	Henry	14	Yorkshire	Labourer
Whyte	William	23	Perthshire	Farm Labourer
Whyte	Peter	21	Perthshire	Farm Labourer
Whyte	James	19	Perthshire	Farm Labourer
Whyte	Robert	14	Perthshire	Farm Labourer
Young	James	30	Lanarkshire	Millwright
Zinckgraf [Linkgraf]	Charles A.	27	Germany	Schoolmaster
Single Women				

Surname	*Given Name*	*Age*	*Location*	*Occupation/ Notes*
~~Anderson~~	~~Mary A.~~	~~19~~	~~Antrim~~	~~Farm Labourer~~
Baker	Sarah Ann	19	Essex	Dom. Servant
Baldwin	Emma	20	Middlesex	Dom. Servant
Beck	Mary E.	19	Armagh	Dom. Servant
Beesley	Mary	26	Lanarkshire	Dom. Servant
Blakeley	Jane	20	Down	Dom. Servant
Crawley	Martha	23	Middlesex	Housekeeper
Duggin	Ellen	28	Middlesex	Dressmaker
Ellenberger	Elise Katharina [Maria]	24	Germany	Dom. Servant
Esselborn	Gertrude	18	Germany	Dom. Servant
Falloon	Elizabeth	20	Tyrone	Dom. Servant
Falloon	Sarah	23	Armagh	Dom, Servant
	Mary	25	Armagh	Dom. Servant
Gardner	Elizabeth	22	Fifeshire	Dom. Servant
Hall	Eliza	24	Armagh	Dom. Servant
Hutcheson	Margaret	21	Armagh	Dom. Servant
Hunt	Ann J.	30	Kent	Cook
Irvine	Ann Jane	22	Armagh	Dom. Servant
Johnson	Sarah	21	Gloucestershire	Dom. Servant

Johnston	Margaret A	26	Yorkshire	Dom. Servant
Kippenberger [listed as Lippenberger]	Gertrude	17	Germany	Dom. Servant
Kippenberger [listed as Lippenberger]	Katherine	15	Germany	Dom. Servant
Lacey	Annie	25	Cork	Dom. Servant
Loney	Jane	15	Armagh	Dom. Servant
Loney	Ann	17	Armagh	Dom. Servant
McKinlay	Margaret	19	Lanarkshire	Dairy Maid
Morris	Mary Ann	31	Norfolk	Dressmaker
Morris	Catherine T.	8	Norfolk	
Newman	Agnes	27	Middlesex	Dom. Servant
Ruddock	Jane	19	Armagh	Dom. Servant
Schmieh	Dorothea	26	Germany	Dom. Servant
Schwartz	Henrietta	17	Germany	Dom. Servant
Schwartz	Barbara	19	Germany	Dom. Servant
Scott	Agnes	13	Lanarkshire	Dom. Servant
Shinn	Mary A.	24	Middlesex	Laundress
Seyb	Catherine	23	Germany	Dom. Servant
Symington	Margaret	21	Lanarkshire	Dairymaid
Tisch	Christina	55	Germany	Dom. Servant
Vallance	Mary E.	31	Devonshire	Housekeeper *Matron on board*
Watts	Elizabeth	20	Wiltshire	Dom. Servant *Travelled with Thorne*
Whyte	Margaret	17	Perthshire	Dom. Servant
Young	Jane	26	Lanarkshire	Dom. Servant
Young	Janet	33	Lanarkshire	Dom. Servant

Unconfirmed Passengers				
Surname	*Given Name*	*Age*	*Location*	*Occupation/ Notes*

?	Arnold		Germany	*Notecard from Meng Documents*
Tissol	Francis		Switzerland	*Lyttelton Times 4/2/1864*

Bibliography

1. wallace Record - Sebastopol built New Glasgow. at <http://db.library.queensu.ca/dbtw-wpd/exec/dbtwpub.dll?AC=GET_RECORD&XC=/dbtw-wpd/exec/dbtwpub.dll&BU=http%3A%2F%2Fdb.library.queensu.ca%2Fmarmus%2Fwallace%2F&TN=wallace&SN=AUTO10944&SE=1145&RN=0&MR=20&TR=0&TX=1000&ES=1&CS=1&XP=&RF=Short+List&EF=Basic+Record+Form&DF=walful&RL=0&EL=1&DL=0&NP=3&ID=&MF=mymsg.ini&MQ=&TI=0&DT=&ST=0&IR=2865&NR=0&NB=0&SV=0&SS=0&BG=bccee2&FG=008080&QS=index&OEX=ISO-8859-1&OEH=ISO-8859-1>
2. McKENZIE, GEORGE ROGERS - Dictionary of Canadian Biography Online. at <http://www.biographi.ca/EN/009004-119.01-e.php?id_nbr=5148>
3. Ships - Sebastopol details. at <http://users.xplornet.com/~shipping/ShipsS.htm>
4. What is a Clipper Ship? | Marine Insight. at <http://www.marineinsight.com/marine/life-at-sea/maritime-history/what-is-a-clipper-ship-2/>
5. Wikipedia contributors. Siege of Sevastopol (1854–1855). *Wikipedia, the free encyclopedia* (2012). at <http://en.wikipedia.org/w/index.php?title=Siege_of_Sevastopol_(1854%E2%80%931855)&oldid=496518931>
6. Government of Canada, C. H. Ship Information Database. (1996). at <http://www.pro.rcip-chin.gc.ca/bd-dl/nav-ship-eng.jsp?emu=en.vessel:/Proxapp/ws/vessel/public/vessel/Record&upp=0&rpp=10&m=5&w=NATIVE%28%27NAME+%3D+%27%27SEBASTOPOL%27%27%27%29&r=1>
7. The Kidston Family — Friends of Glasgow Necropolis. at <http://www.glasgownecropolis.org/profiles/the-kidston-family/>
8. Full text of 'English ruling cases'. at <http://www20.us.archive.org/stream/englishrulingcas14camp/englishrulingcas14camp_djvu.txt>
9. Wikipedia contributors. Packet ship. *Wikipedia, the free encyclopedia* (2012). at <http://en.wikipedia.org/w/index.php?title=Packet_ship&oldid=481049374>
10. Wikipedia contributors. New Zealand Company. *Wikipedia, the free encyclopedia* (2012). at <http://en.wikipedia.org/w/index.php?title=New_Zealand_Company&oldid=491507428>
11. The Mersey clipper ship - Cossar.co.nz. at <http://www.cossar.co.nz/c-mersey.htm>
12. Taonga, N. Z. M. for C. and H. T. M. Settlement in the provinces: 1853 to 1870. at <http://www.teara.govt.nz/en/history-of-immigration/5>
13. Acland, J. B. A. Shipping papers 'Clontarf, A1': ships regulations and plan. University of Canterbury. Acland. (1855).
14. Shaw, Savill And Albion Company | NZETC. at <http://nzetc.victoria.ac.nz/tm/scholarly/tei-Bre01Whit-t1-body-d5.html>
15. Costs and Wages in Great Britain. at <http://www.rootsweb.ancestry.com/~irlcar2/wages.htm>
16. Purdy, F. On the Earnings of Agricultural Labourers in England and Wales, 1860. *Journal of the Statistical Society of London* **24**, 328–373 (1861).
17. Life at Sea: Museum Victoria. at <http://museumvictoria.com.au/discoverycentre/websites-mini/journeys-australia/1850s70s/life-at-sea/>

18. Diver, M. *The Voyages of the Clontarf.* (Dornie Publishing Company, 2011).
19. SHIPPING INTELLIGENCE. HOBSON'S BAY. 9 July 1859. *The Argus* 4 (1859).
20. Sebastopol, ship from London. 8 July 1859. *Empire* 4 (1859).
21. Sebastopol, cleared out. 13 August 1859. *The Argus* 4 (1859).
22. Advertising - Mr Richard Paling. 14 July 1859. *The Argus* 7 (1859).
23. Advertising - food. 18 July 1859. *The Argus* 2 (1859).
24. SHIPS LOADING FOR THE AUSTRALIAN COLONIES. AT LONDON. 11 June 1859. *Empire* 4 (1859).
25. WATER POLICE COURT. WEDNESDAY. *The Sydney Morning Herald* 3 (1859).
26. MERCANTILE AND MONEY ARTICLE. Monday, Evening. 16 August 1859. *The Sydney Morning Herald* 5 (1859).
27. COMMERCIAL. Empire Office, Saturday Evening. *Empire* 4 (1859).
28. Advertising - Bowden and Threkeld Sebastopol sale. 18 October 1859. *Empire* 6 (1859).
29. COMMERCIAL INTELLIGENCE. The Argus Office, Tuesday Evening. 26 October 1859. *The Argus* 4 (1859).
30. Original Correspondence. - Wreck of the Barque Sebastopol. 3 April 1860. *Wellington Independent* 3 (1860).
31. Great Lakes & Seaway Shipping News ARCHIVE. at <http://www.boatnerd.com/news/archive/9-04.htm>
32. Wikipedia contributors. Inkerman and Cerisoles Minesweepers. *Wikipedia, the free encyclopedia* (2012). at <http://en.wikipedia.org/w/index.php?title=Inkerman_and_Cerisoles_Minesweepers&oldid=499082565>
33. Chinese in Guyana: Their Roots. at <http://www.rootsweb.ancestry.com/~guycigtr/>
34. Mystery1859. at <http://freepages.genealogy.rootsweb.ancestry.com/~ourstuff/Mystery.htm>
35. Chinese in Guyana: Their Roots. at <http://www.rootsweb.ancestry.com/~guycigtr/>
36. Shipping Intelligence. - Sebastopol for Callao 1863. 22 July 1863. *Lyttelton Times* 4 (1863).
37. Callao To Valparaiso. 10 January 1871. *North Otago Times* 2 (1871).
38. Wikipedia contributors. Cape Horn. *Wikipedia, the free encyclopedia* (2012). at <http://en.wikipedia.org/w/index.php?title=Cape_Horn&oldid=500311999>
39. McLachlan, J. Abstract of A Log Kept by John McLachlan on His Voyage to New Zealand in the Ship Sebastopol. 2 January 1862. ARC 1900.4 Canterbury Museum. (1862).
40. Wikipedia contributors. John McLachlan. *Wikipedia, the free encyclopedia* (2012). at <http://en.wikipedia.org/w/index.php?title=John_McLachlan&oldid=492048499>
41. Wikipedia contributors. Bay of Biscay. *Wikipedia, the free encyclopedia* (2012). at <http://en.wikipedia.org/w/index.php?title=Bay_of_Biscay&oldid=506197476>
42. Shipping Intelligence - Sebastopol arrival 1861. 18 December 1861. *Lyttelton Times* 4 (1861).
43. Papers Past — Lyttelton Times — 21 June 1862 — Page 6 Advertisements Column 4. (1862). at <http://paperspast.natlib.govt.nz/cgi-bin/paperspast?a=d&d=LT18620621.2.15.4>
44. *Christchurch Parish Records. Christchurch City Libraries.*
45. Probate: McFARLIN Thomas - On board 'Sebastopol' - from C. Down. (1862). at <http://www.archway.archives.govt.nz/ViewFullItem.do?code=22387747>
46. Papers Past — Press — 7 August 1869 — ELLESMERE PLOUGHING MATCH. (1869). at <http://paperspast.natlib.govt.nz/cgi-bin/paperspast?a=d&cl=search&d=CHP18690807.2.10&srpos=39&e=-------10--31----0%22william+brough%22-->

47. Papers Past — Ashburton Guardian — 26 June 1907 — DEATH. (1907). at <http://paperspast.natlib.govt.nz/cgi-bin/paperspast?a=d&cl=search&d=AG19070626.2.10&srpos=1&e=-------10--1----0%22william+brough%22-->
48. Cemetery Record Enquiry - William Brough. at <http://www.adc.govt.nz/cemeteryRecords/46%5C36.html>
49. Papers Past — Star — 1 May 1900 — MAGISTERIAL. (1900). at <http://paperspast.natlib.govt.nz/cgi-bin/paperspast?a=d&cl=search&d=TS19000501.2.42&srpos=15&e=-------10--11----0%22michael+cassin%22-->
50. Christchurch City Council Cemeteries Database Results Details. at <http://librarydata.christchurch.org.nz/Cemeteries/interment.asp?id=127159>
51. Papers Past — Star — 6 October 1879 — CHRISTCHURCH. This Day. (1879). at <http://paperspast.natlib.govt.nz/cgi-bin/paperspast?a=d&cl=search&d=TS18791006.2.22.1&srpos=1&e=-------10--1----0%22henry+eckhoff%22-->
52. Obituary. Fabling. 30 December 1899. *Ellesmere Guardian* 3 (1899).
53. Farmers | NZETC. at <http://nzetc.victoria.ac.nz/tm/scholarly/tei-Cyc03Cycl-t1-body1-d6-d106-d2.html>
54. Papers Past — Star — 29 October 1874 — MAGISTERIAL. (1874). at <http://paperspast.natlib.govt.nz/cgi-bin/paperspast?a=d&cl=search&d=TS18741029.2.9&srpos=18&e=-------10--11----0%22cornelius+hickey%22-->
55. Papers Past — Star — 22 May 1900 — BIRTH. (1900). at <http://paperspast.natlib.govt.nz/cgi-bin/paperspast?a=d&cl=search&d=TS19000522.2.25&srpos=3&e=-------10--1----0%22cornelius+hickey%22-->
56. Papers Past — New Zealand Tablet — 31 May 1900 — OBITUARY. (1900). at <http://paperspast.natlib.govt.nz/cgi-bin/paperspast?a=d&cl=search&d=NZT19000531.2.42&srpos=16&e=-------10--11----0%22cornelius+hickey%22-->
57. Papers Past — New Zealand Tablet — 16 May 1907 — MARRIAGES. (1907). at <http://paperspast.natlib.govt.nz/cgi-bin/paperspast?a=d&cl=search&d=NZT19070516.2.33&srpos=2&e=-------10--1----0%22cornelius+hickey%22-->
58. Press | NZETC - Kerr. at <http://nzetc.victoria.ac.nz/tm/scholarly/tei-Cyc03Cycl-t1-body1-d7-d1-d14.html>
59. Farmers | NZETC - Ligget. at <http://nzetc.victoria.ac.nz/tm/scholarly/tei-Cyc03Cycl-t1-body1-d4-d11-d2.html>
60. 1918.December.Lyttelton.Times.BMD. at <http://homepages.ihug.co.nz/~ashleigh/1870-1908/1918.December.Lyttelton.Times.BMD.html>
61. Great Grandma's Wicker Basket: Jabez Lord's Siblings Who Came to NZ. at <http://greatgrandmaswickerbasket.blogspot.co.nz/2012/05/jabez-lords-siblings-who-came-to-nz.html>
62. Old Colonists | NZETC - May. at <http://nzetc.victoria.ac.nz/tm/scholarly/tei-Cyc03Cycl-t1-body1-d4-d27-d3.html>
63. Power Family - Power Family. at <http://www.powerfamily.co.nz/>
64. Farmers | NZETC - Rainey. at <http://nzetc.victoria.ac.nz/tm/scholarly/tei-Cyc03Cycl-t1-body1-d6-d6-d2.html>
65. [Weedons] | NZETC. at <http://nzetc.victoria.ac.nz/tm/scholarly/tei-Cyc03Cycl-t1-body1-d6-d23-d1.html>

66. A L Powys' Life. at <http://www.tim.ukpub.net/Manuscripts/art_powys_biog.html>
67. Zuppicich, Antonio | NZETC. at <http://nzetc.victoria.ac.nz/tm/scholarly/tei-Cyc03Cycl-t1-body1-d4-d7-d26.html>
68. Papers Past — Lyttelton Times — 3 June 1863 — SHIPPING INTELLIGENCE. (1863). at <http://paperspast.natlib.govt.nz/cgi-bin/paperspast?a=d&cl=search&d=LT18630603.2.13&srpos=20&e=-------10--11----0testimonial+sebastopol-->
69. Papers Past — Daily Southern Cross — 25 April 1863 — ENGLISH SHIPPING. (1863). at <http://paperspast.natlib.govt.nz/cgi-bin/paperspast?a=d&cl=search&d=DSC18630425.2.21.4&srpos=2&e=-------10--1----0needles+sebastopol-->
70. Wikipedia contributors. The Needles. *Wikipedia, the free encyclopedia* (2012). at <http://en.wikipedia.org/w/index.php?title=The_Needles&oldid=504608445>
71. Taonga, N. Z. M. for C. and H. T. M. Gardner, Margaret. at <http://www.teara.govt.nz/en/biographies/1g3/1>
72. Meng Family in Hohen-Sülzen. Letter to Karl Meng (unpublished), 1864. Rights: G. Fraser and S. Baker. Translated by Klaus Nasterlack, 2012. (1863).
73. Inquest for Charles John Galbraith, surgeon on board the Sebastopol. Archives New Zealand. 1863. (1863).
74. Papers Past — Lyttelton Times — 23 May 1863 — SHIPPING INTELLIGENCE. (1863). at <http://paperspast.natlib.govt.nz/cgi-bin/paperspast?a=d&cl=search&d=LT18630523.2.10&srpos=9&e=23-05-1863-23-05-1863--10--1----0sebastopol-->
75. Papers Past — Lyttelton Times — 30 May 1863 — TOWN AND COUNTRY NEWS. Elizabeth Baxter. at <http://paperspast.natlib.govt.nz/cgi-bin/paperspast?a=d&d=LT18630530.2.9&e=-------10--1--on--2%22walter+brain%22-->
76. Lyttelton. 1 June 1863. *Otago Daily Times* 4 (1863).
77. Papers Past — Lyttelton Times — 8 April 1863 — LYTTELTON MUNICIPAL COUNCIL. (1863). at <http://paperspast.natlib.govt.nz/cgi-bin/paperspast?a=d&cl=search&d=LT18630408.2.12&srpos=2&e=-------10--1----0marshman+sebastopol-->
78. Shipping Intelligence. - Tisch leaving NZ. 3 May 1862. *Press* 6 (1862).
79. Leininger Geschichtsblätter. Published Germany, 1910. Translated by Klaus Nasterlack, 2012. (1910).
80. Arnst, I. and S. Talk with German Researchers Ian and Stella Arnst. May 2012. (2012).
81. Suicide Of Dr. Galbraith. 3 June 1863. *Lyttelton Times* 3 (1863).
82. Charles John Galbraith birth - Search Results—FamilySearch.org — Free Family History and Genealogy Records. at <https://familysearch.org/pal:/MM9.1.1/J3KW-CLW>
83. John Galbraith and Charlotte Wimberley marriage - Search Results—FamilySearch.org — Free Family History and Genealogy Records. at <https://familysearch.org/pal:/MM9.1.1/NJJ3-D9X>
84. Dow, D. The drunk docs who didn't dry out - New Zealand Doctor. at <http://www.nzdoctor.co.nz/in-print/2010/november-2010/3-november-2010/the-drunk-docs-who-didn%E2%80%99t-dry-out.aspx>
85. Probate: GALBRAITH Charles John - Lyttelton Harbour - 'Sebastopol'. (1863). at <http://www.archway.archives.govt.nz/ViewFullItem.do?code=22387769>
86. FreeBMD - Search - Death of Charles Gray M Galbraith. at <http://www.freebmd.org.uk/cgi/search.pl?start=1873&end=1873&sq=1&eq=1&type=Deaths&vol=5a&pgno=221&jsexec=1&mono=0&v=MTM0OTY1OTYxMzpjNT

RiMjAxMzk3NmRiN2EwOTNkMGJmYThlNGYzY2FlNjFmMTA4NDZi&searchd ef=given%3Dcharles%26db%3Dbmd_1348835454%26type%3DDeaths%26sq%3D 1%26v%3DMTM0OTY1OTYwMjpiM2FlMTdlMGRhYTRmMTBkMjhjODg0MT AxYjZhOTM1MDM0NzYzYmVk%26eq%3D4%26surname%3Dgalbraith&action= Find>

87. Wikipedia contributors. Edward VII. *Wikipedia, the free encyclopedia* (2012). at <http://en.wikipedia.org/w/index.php?title=Edward_VII&oldid=500972117>
88. Papers Past — Lyttelton Times — 15 July 1863 — FESTIVITIES. (1863). at <http://paperspast.natlib.govt.nz/cgi-bin/paperspast?a=d&d=LT18630715.2.3&cl=search&srpos=5&e=-04-1863--08-1863--10-LT-1----0sebastopol+guns-->
89. Farmers | NZETC - Anderson. at <http://nzetc.victoria.ac.nz/tm/scholarly/tei-Cyc03Cycl-t1-body1-d4-d14-d2.html>
90. William Edgar Billens. at <http://hayleyfamily.familytreeguide.com/getperson.php?personID=I1126&tree=T1 &PHPSESSID=25b31bddb37d12195040e775a1947f5d>
91. Papers Past — Timaru Herald — 3 September 1873 — INQUEST. (1873). at <http://paperspast.natlib.govt.nz/cgi-bin/paperspast?a=d&d=THD18730903.2.15&e=-------10--1----0-->
92. Birth, Death and Marriage Historical Records. at <https://bdmhistoricalrecords.dia.govt.nz/Home/>
93. Hills, D. and H. *Settling near the Styx River*. (D A & H J Hills, 2006).
94. Great Grandma's Wicker Basket: The Ellenberger Family. at <http://greatgrandmaswickerbasket.blogspot.co.nz/2012/05/ellenberger-family.html>
95. Falloon - Reid - Marraige - New Zealand - Falloon - Family History & Genealogy Message Board - Ancestry.com. at <http://boards.ancestry.com/thread.aspx?mv=flat&m=46&p=surnames.falloon>
96. Old Colonists | NZETC - Gardner. at <http://nzetc.victoria.ac.nz/tm/scholarly/tei-Cyc03Cycl-t1-body1-d4-d14-d3.html>
97. Canterbury Heritage: Looters Ransack Historic Site. at <http://canterburyheritage.blogspot.co.nz/2009/03/looters-ransack-historic-site.html>
98. ChristchurchStreetNames-I-K.pdf. at <http://christchurchcitylibraries.com/Heritage/PlaceNames/ChristchurchStreetNames -I-K.pdf>
99. Mr. James Purvis Jameson | NZETC. at <http://nzetc.victoria.ac.nz/tm/scholarly/tei-Cyc03Cycl-t1-body1-d3-d9-d5.html>
100. Mr. William Jameson, F.I.A.N.Z | NZETC. at <http://nzetc.victoria.ac.nz/tm/scholarly/tei-Cyc03Cycl-t1-body1-d3-d13-d11.html>
101. Little, Roy. *Pride in Family - The Kippenbergers*. (April 20).
102. Glentui — (Run 145) | NZETC. at <http://nzetc.victoria.ac.nz/tm/scholarly/tei-AclEarl-t1-body-d3-d14.html>
103. Cust / West Eyreton (Mairaki) Cemetery. *Hunting Kiwis* at <http://genealogyjourno.wordpress.com/rural-cemeteries-of-canterbury-new-zealand/cust-west-eyreton-public-cemetery/>
104. Great Grandma's Wicker Basket: The Meng Family. at <http://greatgrandmaswickerbasket.blogspot.co.nz/2012/05/meng-family.html>
105. Pollock, William | NZETC. at <http://nzetc.victoria.ac.nz/tm/scholarly/tei-Cyc04Cycl-t1-body1-d3-d11-d2.html>
106. Southbridge | NZETC. at <http://nzetc.victoria.ac.nz/tm/scholarly/tei-Cyc03Cycl-t1-body1-d6-d19.html>
107. Holy Trinity Anglican Church ,Avonside, Transcript of Baptismal Registar 1856-

1880. (1982).
108. Papers Past — Star — 4 August 1908 — DEATHS. (1908). at <http://paperspast.natlib.govt.nz/cgi-bin/paperspast?a=d&d=TS19080804.2.43>
109. RootsWeb's WorldConnect Project: Thorne family from Newnham, GLS to Canterbury, New Zealand. at <http://wc.rootsweb.ancestry.com/cgi-bin/igm.cgi?op=GET&db=thojan09&id=I5>
110. Corrigan, B. Tisch. Email from Barbara Corrigan. 11 June 2012. (2012).
111. Elizabeth Grace Watts. *geni_family_tree* at <http://www.geni.com/people/Elizabeth-Grace-Watts/6000000010415050862>
112. Halkett | NZETC - William Whyte. at <http://nzetc.victoria.ac.nz/tm/scholarly/tei-Cyc03Cycl-t1-body1-d6-d28.html>
113. Search Results—FamilySearch.org — Free Family History and Genealogy Records - Henry Widdop. at <https://familysearch.org/pal:/MM9.1.1/N4W6-FJ5>
114. Hartwig, Craig. Zinckgraf. (2012).
115. Lyttelton. - Unclaimed letters. 24 April 1862. *Lyttelton Times* 3 (1862).

www.ingramcontent.com/pod-product-compliance
Lightning Source LLC
Chambersburg PA
CBHW050652160426
43194CB00010B/1906